Economics For Business Environment

# Orangebooks Publication

1st Floor, Rajhans Arcade, Mall Road, Kohka, Bhilai, Chhattisgarh 490020

Website: **www.orangebooks.in**

© **Copyright, 2024, Author**

All rights reserved. No part of this book may be reproduced, stored in a retrieval system, or transmitted, in any form by any means, electronic, mechanical, magnetic, optical, chemical, manual, photocopying, recording or otherwise, without the prior written consent of its writer.

**First Edition, 2024**
**ISBN:** 978-93-6554-580-7

# ECONOMICS
## —— FOR ——
# BUSINESS ENVIRONMENT

Dr. Kaushik Banerjee
Dr. Sudipta Adhikary  Mr. Subham Chatterjee

OrangeBooks Publication
www.orangebooks.in

# Index

## Chapter - 1
Introduction _____ 1
- ➤ Business Nature _____ 1
- ➤ Business Objectives _____ 5
- ➤ Characteristics Of Business Environment _____ 10
- ➤ Environmental Analysis _____ 11
- ➤ Social Issues _____ 15
- ➤ Economic Issues Pertaining To India _____ 20
- ➤ Social Responsibility Of Business _____ 28
- ➤ Internal Environment _____ 41
- ➤ External Environment _____ 42

## Chapter - 2
Macroeconomic Variables _____ 64
- ➤ National Income: _____ 64
- ➤ Monetary Policy _____ 68
- ➤ Fiscal Policy _____ 84
- ➤ Industrial Policy 1991 _____ 93

## Chapter 3
Banking Infrastructure For Economic Development _ 106
- ➤ Reserve Bank Of India _____ 106
- ➤ RBI And Monetary Policy _____ 111
- ➤ Commercial Banking _____ 114

## Chapter 4
## Privatization, Globalization And Foreign Trade Policy _____ 127

- ➤ Privatizazion _____ 127
- ➤ Privatisation In India – An Inside Look _____ 133
- ➤ Disinvestment _____ 136
- ➤ Globalization _____ 141
- ➤ Foreign Trade Policy In India _____ 159

## Chapter 5
## International Organizations _____ 167

- ➤ GATT _____ 167
- ➤ WTO – Status _____ 169
- ➤ World Bank _____ 175

## Chapter 6
## Human Resource Development And Sustainable Development _____ 183

- ➤ Human Resource Management _____ 183
- ➤ Training And Development _____ 204
- ➤ HR Accounting And Audit _____ 207
- ➤ Sustainable Development _____ 217

# Chapter - 1
# Introduction

**CHAPTER CONTENT**

Business nature

Business Objectives

Characteristics of Business Environment

Environmental analysis

Social Issues

Economic issues pertaining to India

Social responsibility of business

Internal environment of business

External environment of business

## Business Nature

Generally speaking, "business" refers to the creation and application of economic values in society. The phrase is typically used to describe a subset of economic activity whose main goal is to efficiently supply products and services to society. It is also used in the economics and business dealings of organizations with different goals. Business primarily refers to all of an organization's profit-seeking endeavors that produce commodities and services required by the economy. It is the main engine of a country's economy, working to raise living standards for all.

A business is any entity that distributes goods or renders services to consumers who are also members of the community. A business's goal is to meet the requirements of its clients as long as they can afford to do so. The term "business" can be defined as "the coordinated endeavor of individuals to generate goods and services, market these goods and services, and obtain compensation for this endeavor." "Those human activities which involves production or purchase of goods with the object of selling them at a profit margin" is a useful definition of business. There are a number of approaches to understand business, some of which are as follows:

It is expansive and open to utilizing a variety of activities. It includes buying, selling, producing, processing, marketing goods and services, as well as trade, warehousing, banking and finance, insurance, and advertising.

The primary driver of company is profit. It is made very obvious that making money is the primary goal of all company endeavors. Profit is an excess of business that is generated and given to the company's owners. Employing businesses are required to pay their employees' salary. People give money to businesses in order to be retained. Retain is the company's profit. The investor receives something for assuming the risk. Profit acts as both the driving force behind the investor's service and management of the company and serves as a catalyst for the enterprise's expansion and survival. Profit is a common motivator for business owners in all types of organizations, as it serves as a gauge of the enterprise's overall performance.

Profit is a metric used to assess productivity and business efficiency at the managerial level. It supports strategic managers in making wise judgments and taking appropriate action, which leads to effectiveness since they can integrate and make use of the resources at their disposal and maintain the organization's growth.

The market value of company shares, sales volume, capital utilized, and profit percentage are the metrics used to describe business efficiency.

External investors are keen to ascertain the company's profitability and evaluate their commitment of funds, since only within the business entity can funds be utilized effectively.

Different individuals and personalities have given their own interpretations of what business is. Peter F. Drucker has made several observations on businesses. The following is a list of his conclusions:

People are the ones who establish and run businesses. A team of individuals tasked with making decisions that will decide an organization's chances of success or failure, of surviving the market or finally going out of business.

A business's organized attempts to provide customers with goods and services while making a profit can be summed up as business. Companies differ in size depending on how many people they employ or how much money they make. However, the goal of every firm is the same: to make money.

A business's goals extend beyond making money. It is a significant institution in society for the following reasons:

- It is necessary for the provision of products and services
- Increasing employment prospects;
- Providing a higher standard of living;
- Supporting the nation's economic expansion.

Thus, it is acknowledged that business plays a critical role. There would be no society without commerce. The need of business to society cannot be overstated.

## Business Now

The corporate world of today is dynamic. Change is the finest word to characterize today's business, if there is one. In order to stay in the market, this shift forces the companies to spend a lot of money on research and development (R&D).

For businesses, mass production and mass marketing are standard operating procedures. In 1969–70, there were just three enterprises with an annual sales of Rs. 100 crore a piece. These days, the number has increased by hundreds.

**Diversification is a hallmark of modern company, and it can be:**

Focused diversification is the process of introducing new, related goods and services.

Horizontal Diversification: This is the process of offering current clients new, unrelated goods or services.

Conglomerate diversification is the process of introducing new, unconnected goods and services.

### 21$^{st}$ Century Business

There won't be big companies with a lot of employees. These will be "Mini" companies. The 21st century will see a knowledge-based business environment, meaning managers won't have to spend their days shuffling papers and moving files

The majority of that labour will be handled by information technology. Businesses will get stale. There will be no longer be a linear hierarchy between the manager and the boss, with authority moving down and obedience moving up. Workers won't have set positions. Most of the positions are for a period of two to five years. Pay will be determined by how much each employee contributes to the company.

## Business Objectives

Profit: Any business's main objective is to turn a profit.

Growth: Over time, a business should expand in all ways.

Power: Companies has a great deal of resources at their disposal. These assets offer significant political and economic power.

Employee growth and satisfaction: People are the business. Enlightened commercial businesses have always aimed to provide for the development and well-being of their employees.

Goods and Services: Reliability in goods creates brand loyalty, which is essential for success.

Market Leadership: The secret to carving out a place for oneself in the market is innovation.

Joy of creation: New concepts and inventions are given shape and turned into practical goods and services by means of business strategies.

Service to society: Businesses have a number of responsibilities to society as it is a part of it.

The business environment

Environmental Types

The environment is made up of elements including the government, supplier, competitors, technology, and socioeconomics. There are two other factors that have a big impact on company. The two are the global environment and the physical or natural environment.

Technological Setting

Technology is defined as the methodical application of organized knowledge, such as science, to real-world problems. Technological advancements occur quickly, therefore entrepreneurs must constantly be on the lookout for opportunities to integrate new technologies into their operations.

**Financial Situation**

The corporate world and its economic environment are closely related. The economic environment provides business with all of its inputs, and business units' output is absorbed by business.

**Political Scene**

It speaks of the power that the three political branches the legislature, the executive branch, and the judiciary have over how corporate operations are developed, shaped, and controlled. A politically secure yet dynamic atmosphere is essential for the expansion of businesses.

**The Natural World**

Man's economic endeavour, business, is nevertheless determined by the laws of nature. An intriguing subject to research is how much business depends on nature and how the two are related.

Worldwide or worldwide context

Indian businesses are now compelled to consider business matters globally as a result of liberalization. To thrive in the global environment, managerial strategies and business responses need to be adjusted.

**Cultural and Social Environment**

It speaks to how people view wealth and employment, the importance of marriage, families, and religion, as well as ethical concerns and how socially conscious businesses should be.

**Environment - Commercial Connections**

Technological, political-legal, economic, social-cultural, global, and natural variables all have a role in the creation of business. This network of relationships between company and its surroundings shares three characteristics.

- There is a symbolic relationship among the environmental components and between business and its surroundings. Put another way, business is affected by its surroundings and, in turn, will have some impact over outside factors. Likewise, the political and legal landscape shapes the economic landscape and vice versa.

- There is movement to these environmental factors. They, along with company, continue to evolve as the years pass.

- The third characteristic is that a certain company might not be able to alter its surroundings on its own. However, business will have the ability to influence the environment in its favour along with other companies.

The value of environmental research

The following are some advantages of studying the environment:

- Creation of the company's long-term policies and broad strategies.

- Creating plans of action to address new developments in technology.
- To predict how socioeconomic shifts on a national and global scale would affect the stability of the company.
- Examining the tactics used by rivals and developing successful countermeasures.

**There are four consecutive steps in the analysis:**

### Examining

It entails broad monitoring of all environmental variables and their interactions with the goal of detecting environmental change that is actually occurring as well as early warning signs of potential change.

### Observing

It entails keeping tabs on patterns in the environment, occurrences in succession, or activity streams. It usually entails tracking signs or indicators that are found when scanning the environment.

### Predicting

Making strategic decisions necessitates seeing forward. It goes without saying that forecasting is a crucial component of environmental study. The goal of forecasting is to create believable estimates of the pace, extent, and direction of environmental change.

## Evaluation

Understanding the environment—the emphasis of scanning, monitoring, and forecasting—moves to understanding what the understanding implies for the organization in the assessment process. The goal of assessment is to provide answers to queries like what are the main environmental challenges and how they affect the organization.

## Characteristics Of Business Environment

The main obstacles, chances, threats, and vulnerabilities that a business faces will reveal the features of the business environment.

The main components of the business environment include many events and factors. These are impacted by several organizational departmental sources. These circumstances don't exist in a vacuum; they give rise to a whole new set of influences that interact with one another. It has a broad impact on the corporate environment, yet it is challenging to change an organization. All of these elements must be taken into account since environment analysis is intricate, rigorous, and extremely challenging for functional managers and other high-ranking personnel inside the company to understand.

The business and corporate environment is always changing and evolving in a number of ways. Factors from both the macro and micro environments affect company. It has an effect on altering the business environment. A dynamic environment is naturally adaptable. Change is to blame for this; a strategic manager can create both short- and long-term goals and frame strategy.

A strategic observer is able to form and observe various characters that are present in the surroundings. A strategic observer can spot a specific shift or the most recent advancement in the company. It could be seen differently by various organization watchers. When the development occurs, these things are commonly observed. While most people are pleased to embrace it and see it as a chance for the business, occasionally it may even be seen as a danger.

The environment has a broad influence on businesses. The impact of the environment is a crucial component for strategists to analyze trends and make the right decisions at the right moments. The organization is impacted if the strategist fails to make the right choice at the right moment. An organization's ability to survive, expand, be profitable, and evolve depends crucially on both micro and macro aspects of the business environment. The impact of the environment gives the business additional dimensions.

## Environmental Analysis

A strategist should be knowledgeable about the company's resource capacities and how to use its limited resources most efficiently. Analyzing the shifting pattern and its effects on business is the goal of environment analysis. It also takes into account a chance and a period of time to plan ahead, anticipate corporate goals, and utilize firm resources to their fullest potential. These elements aid in the formation, development, and dissemination of early warning systems to avert hazards or the creation of tactics that can convert threats into advantages within the established system. It gives a clear indication of the company's future and an evaluation of what is expected of it.

Environment analysis is defined by Clifton Garvin as follows: "Positive trends in the environment breed complacency." That emphasizes a fundamental idea: change presents both opportunities and challenges. Analysis, diagnosis, and managerial decisions that are likely to be made for the company's improvement are all included in business environment analysis. It shortens the procedure and eases the time constraints that the company's managers and board of directors must deal with. However, there are instances where strategic managers disregard the environment analysis and how it affects changes to the firm, even while they are prepared to deal with future issues. Consequently, the strategic managers can focus on how the environment affects the company or organization.

## Environmental analysis often aims to achieve the following three main objectives:

The strategist must be able to understand the existing and anticipated changes from environmental analysis, as well as where they fit into the corporate environment. The current environment is crucial for strategists to understand since it affects the organization most. The strategist must simultaneously adopt and take into account a long-term outlook for the future.

Strategic inputs are essentially what environment analysis offers to strategic decision makers. It is insufficient to analyses the environment and is not just a collection of data. The organization should be able to use the information the strategist gathers to inform its strategic decision-making.

The fundamental instrument for creating, facilitating, and fostering strategic thinking within an organization is environment analysis. Usually, it is an abundant reservoir of skills and concepts that comprehend the background and scope of the corporate entity. It ought to focus on the potential, growth, progress, and difficulties of the present.

A component of SWOT analysis is environment influence. Strengths, Weaknesses, Opportunities, and Threats are shortened to SWOT. Both opportunities and threats are a part of the business's external environment. The internal environment of the firm include both strengths and weaknesses. Below is an outline of these factors:

**Strength**

IS an organization's or company's innate resource capability that may be leveraged to obtain a competitive edge over rivals in the market. Strength, for instance, is the ability needed for creativity and research, which aids in the development of advanced talents that are subsequently utilized to obtain new materials, new products, and new clients. We are able to acquire competitive advantages in the business in this way.

**Weakness**

An organizational weakness is an innate limitation, constraint, or issue. It causes the business or organization to have strategic disadvantages. For instance, an over reliance on one supplier in the market during a crisis may pose a risk to a manufacturing company.

**Opportunity**

An opportunity is a beneficial circumstance in the company organization's surroundings that allows it to fortify its position and gather resources. Consider the rise in the company's goods and services as a result of consumer demand. It is the company's finest chance to provide clients with goods and services.

**Threat**

A threat is an undesirable circumstance in the surroundings of a business organization that puts the organization at risk or damages it. A developing powerful competitor in the market, for instance, could present fierce competition for established businesses in the trade, industry, and business.

An organisation shouldn't always go after the most profitable prospects. Rather, by finding a match between the organization's strengths and impending possibilities, it might have a better chance of creating a competitive edge. Sometimes an organisation can overcome a weakness to position itself to take advantage of a strong opportunity. These elements can be arranged in a matrix to help create strategies that consider the SWOT profile. The TOWS matrix is another name for the SWOT matrix.

Tactics of Business Environment

S-O tactics

W-O tactics

S-T tactics

W-T tactics

S-O strategies: look for opportunities that align well with the company's capabilities.

W-O strategies: capitalise on opportunities by overcoming weaknesses.

S-T strategies: determine how the business may leverage its advantages to lessen its susceptibility to outside dangers.

W-T strategies: create a defence strategy to stop the company's vulnerabilities from rendering it extremely vulnerable to outside threats.

## Social Issues

India's rapid population increase has proven to be a significant barrier to economic development because it tends to offset gains in wealth. Additionally, it has made it necessary to shift scarce resources from channels of production to channels of consumption, resulting in an ever-shrinking resource base for future economic growth. As Gunnar Myrdal so eloquently put it, the majority of South-East Asian nations have entered a key phase of dramatically accelerated population growth and are currently experiencing a true demographic revolution, the scale and speed of which have never been seen before in history. Population control programmes should go hand in hand with economic growth and prosperity, as economic planning will fail to yield noticeable benefits unless this "demographic revolution" is taken into consideration.

**Social Stratification:**

Social stratification refers to the hierarchical arrangement of individuals in a society based on their socio-economic status, which includes wealth, power, and prestige. It leads to the unequal distribution of resources and opportunities among different social groups.

**Characteristics:**

1 **Structured Inequality:** Social stratification is systematic and not random.

2 **Persistence:** Stratification tends to persist across generations.

3 **Universality:** It is a feature of all societies, though the forms and extents vary.

4 **Belief System:** It is supported by a society's belief systems and ideologies that justify the inequalities.

**Dimensions of Stratification:**

1 **Economic Class:** Based on wealth and income.

2 **Social Status:** Reflects prestige and lifestyle.

3 **Power:** Control over resources and decision-making processes.

**Types of Social Stratification:**

1 **Class System:** Open system where social mobility is possible. Classes are based on economic position.

2. **Caste System:** Closed system where social position is inherited and rigid, with little to no mobility.

3. **Estate System:** Historically based on land ownership and hereditary nobility.

4. **Status Hierarchy System:** Based on social prestige rather than purely economic factors.

Theoretical Perspectives on Social Stratification

## 1. Functionalist Theory (e.g., Davis and Moore)

**Main Idea:** Stratification is necessary for the functioning of society.

**Arguments:** Certain positions are more important and require special skills; therefore, rewards motivate individuals to fill these positions.

**Criticism:** Overemphasizes the positive aspects of stratification and neglects the role of power and coercion.

## 2. Conflict Theory (e.g., Karl Marx, Max Weber)

**Main Idea:** Stratification results from the exploitation of one class by another.

**Marx:** Focuses on the economic dimension, with society divided into the bourgeoisie (owners) and proletariat (workers).

**Weber:** Adds dimensions of status and power, arguing that stratification is more complex and includes class, status, and party.

**Criticism:** Can overemphasize economic factors and underplay the role of ideas and values.

## 3. Symbolic Interactionism

**Main Idea:** Examines how social stratification is maintained and experienced through daily interactions and symbols.

**Arguments:** Social status and class are constructed through social interactions, and individuals learn their place in the hierarchy through socialization.

**Criticism:** May overlook larger structural factors and focus too much on individual agency.

Social Mobility

**Definition:** Social mobility refers to the movement of individuals or groups within the social hierarchy, which can be upward or downward.

## Types:

1  **Vertical Mobility:** Moving up or down the socio-economic ladder.

2  **Horizontal Mobility:** Changing positions without altering one's socio-economic status.

3  **Intergenerational Mobility:** Changes in social status between different generations within a family.

4  **Intragenerational Mobility:** Changes in social status within an individual's lifetime.

## Factors Influencing Social Mobility:

1  **Education:** A key factor for upward mobility.

2  **Family Background:** Influences access to resources and opportunities.

3 **Social Networks:** Can provide connections and support for mobility.

4 **Economic and Social Policies:** Government policies can enhance or hinder mobility.

Global Perspectives on Social Stratification.

### 1. Global Inequality:

**High-Income Countries:** Higher levels of wealth and resources, leading to better health, education, and living standards.

**Middle-Income Countries:** Emerging economies with moderate levels of industrialization.

**Low-Income Countries:** Limited industrialization, high levels of poverty, and lower living standards.

### 2. Theories of Global Stratification:

**Modernization Theory:** Suggests that economic development and modernization will lead to the reduction of global inequalities.

**Dependency Theory:** Argues that historical exploitation and colonialism have created unequal economic relationships, leading to persistent global inequality.

**World-Systems Theory:** Posits that the global economy is divided into core, semi-periphery, and periphery countries, creating a structured inequality on a global scale.

# Economic Issues Pertaining To India

## 1  Poverty:

Poverty is a much larger concept than just an economic one. The social structure both causes and maintains the widespread poverty. It's been referred to as "artificial" poverty. In other words, poverty is a condition that society creates. It is multifaceted, encompassing social, political, cultural, and economic facets. But political, social, and cultural regression serve as the foundation for and sustain economic destitution.

Approaches to Poverty: There are two approaches to poverty the nutritional approach and the 'relative deprivation' approach.

The underdeveloped world has embraced the nutritional approach. Here, the need for food is used as a gauge of poverty. Individuals are considered to be below the poverty line if their low income prevents them from consuming the bare minimum amount of food. Individuals who earn less than the federal poverty threshold are classified as impoverished. This is a level of "absolute poverty." Since meeting one's basic food needs is not the main issue, the "relative deprivation" approach has been used to measure poverty in industrialized nations. Here, poverty is defined as the relative deprivation of a segment of the population relative to those who are affluent. In this case, societal injustices are prioritized before dietary needs.

## 2 Problem of Unemployment:

Our existence depends on our ability to work, and unemployment jeopardizes our survival. As McNamara correctly noted, unemployment is not only widespread in the developing world but is also getting worse, particularly in cities. Industrial employment has increased far more slowly than urban population growth, which has been growing at an average yearly pace of nearly 5% in developing nations.

Poverty in India refers to the state where individuals lack sufficient financial resources to meet basic living needs such as food, shelter, healthcare, and education. It is typically measured by income levels, consumption expenditure, and access to essential services.

### Measurement of Poverty:

1. **Poverty Line:** Defined by the government, it represents the minimum income required to meet basic needs. As per recent updates, the poverty line in India is based on consumption expenditure.

2. **Multidimensional Poverty Index (MPI):** Includes indicators across health, education, and living standards, providing a more comprehensive measure of poverty.

### Extent and Trends:

1. **Poverty Rates:** Significant decline over the past few decades, but substantial disparities remain across regions, castes, and urban-rural divides.

2. **Urban vs. Rural Poverty:** Higher poverty rates in rural areas compared to urban areas due to limited access to infrastructure, education, and employment opportunities.

3. **Regional Disparities:** States like Bihar, Uttar Pradesh, and Odisha have higher poverty rates compared to more affluent states like Kerala, Maharashtra, and Gujarat.

## Causes of Poverty in India

**1 Economic Factors:**

**Unemployment and Underemployment:** High rates of unemployment and underemployment, especially in rural areas and among unskilled workers.

**Agrarian Distress:** Dependence on agriculture with low productivity, lack of irrigation facilities, and frequent crop failures.

**Informal Sector:** Large portion of the workforce employed in the informal sector with low wages and lack of social security.

**2 Social Factors:**

**Caste and Gender Discrimination:** Historical and systemic discrimination leading to limited access to education, employment, and resources for marginalized groups.

**Lack of Education:** Low literacy rates and inadequate educational facilities contribute to skill gaps and unemployment.

## 3 Infrastructure and Services:

**Healthcare:** Poor access to healthcare services, leading to high out-of-pocket expenses and health-related poverty traps.

**Sanitation and Housing:** Inadequate housing and sanitation facilities affecting the quality of life and productivity.

## 4 Policy and Governance:

**Ineffective Implementation:** Poor implementation of poverty alleviation programs and corruption.

**Land Reforms:** Incomplete land reforms and lack of land ownership among the rural poor.

## Poverty Alleviation Programs and Initiatives

### 1 Economic and Social Development Programs:

**Mahatma Gandhi National Rural Employment Guarantee Act (MGNREGA):** Provides 100 days of guaranteed wage employment to rural households.

**National Rural Livelihood Mission (NRLM):** Promotes self-employment and organization of rural poor into self-help groups.

**Pradhan Mantri Awas Yojana (PMAY):** Aims to provide affordable housing to the urban and rural poor.

### 2 Education and Skill Development:

**Sarva Shiksha Abhiyan (SSA):** Universalizes elementary education.

**Skill India Mission:** Enhances skill development to improve employability.

### 3  Health and Nutrition:

**Ayushman Bharat:** Provides health insurance coverage to economically vulnerable families.

**Integrated Child Development Services (ICDS):** Addresses child malnutrition and provides healthcare.

### 4  Financial Inclusion:

**Pradhan Mantri Jan Dhan Yojana (PMJDY):** Promotes financial inclusion by ensuring access to financial services.

### Challenges and Future Directions

### 1  Implementation and Monitoring:

Enhancing transparency and accountability in the implementation of poverty alleviation programs.

Utilizing technology for better monitoring and delivery of services.

### 2  Inclusive Growth:

Focusing on inclusive growth that benefits all sections of society, especially marginalized groups.

Promoting rural development and agrarian reforms to boost rural incomes.

## 3  Education and Health:

Improving the quality of education and healthcare services to build human capital.

Addressing malnutrition and health disparities through targeted interventions.

## 4  Employment Generation:

Encouraging entrepreneurship and small businesses to create job opportunities.

Investing in skill development and vocational training to meet market demands.

**Low Per Capita Income:** When it comes to per capita income, India is among the least developed nations. India's GNP per capita estimate, calculated using Purchasing Power Parity, was as low as $1,700 in 1998. This represents approximately 1/17th of the USA's GNP per capita estimate, which was $29,340.

**Unequal Distribution of Wealth and Poverty:** There is an unequal distribution of wealth and income in India. The licence and permit, which were first intended to prevent the concentration of economic power in a few hands, quickly turned into a weapon for generating inequality. It is evident that a small number of businesses were granted licences to make a wide range of goods, including trucks and pins, at a subpar level. This was made feasible by the artificial restriction on capacity expansion that led to the shortage of almost all commodities in India. Everything was available in black, including cement and kerosene, which led to the emergence of a parallel black economy across the nation.

Additionally, there was an unequal distribution of financial resources.

In addition to this, poverty is a significant issue for the Indian economy. According to data from the Planning Commission, 36 percent of Indians were living in poverty in 1993–94. Thus, this estimate of poverty unequivocally demonstrates that large swaths of our society have not benefited from India's more than four decades of economic expansion.

**Dominance of Agriculture:** In 1998, 25% of the GDP came from agriculture. However, almost 65% of Indians still rely on agriculture as their primary source of income. In comparison, just 3% of Americans work in agriculture, which is sufficient for both domestic consumption and international exports. India's poverty is mostly caused by its massive population's reliance on agriculture.

**Rapid Population Growth:** As death rates are down without a matching drop in birth rates, India is experiencing a population boom. The impoverished and the villages are experiencing the fastest rates of population growth.

**Inflation**

While inflation is commonly used to describe a general increase in costs, it actually refers to a persistent increase in prices combined with a decline in the value of the currency.

A 'basket' of commodities is used to estimate inflation by comparing prices at two intervals and accounting for changes in the intrinsic basket. As a result, the inflation rate varies based on the commodities basket that is chosen. Consumer inflation, producer inflation, GDP deflators, and price indices are the most often used metrics. Therefore, 10% inflation would occur if the overall price was, say, $100 in 2000 and $110 in 2001. Thus, it may be concluded that money loses purchasing power when there is inflation.

**Causes of inflation in India**

Rise in price of agricultural products: Agriculture in India still depends heavily on the gifts of nature to a large extent nowadays. This causes fluctuations in agricultural output. India's output per acre is quite low due to tiny private holdings. Because they lack access to modern technology, peasants are more susceptible to natural disasters. Additionally, they lack a professional approach, which prevents them from choosing the best crop based on the market demand and climate. The end outcome of all this is variations in agricultural productivity. Their prices dramatically increase when the nation's output diminishes. An increase in the price of agricultural goods is automatically reflected in the general price index since they carry a significant amount of weight in the wholesale price index.

For instance, because industrial workers spend a large portion of their earnings on food, increases in food prices cause them to buy other commodities, the prices of which climb when agricultural produce is scarce.

Essential Goods Stockpiling: Large farmers and middlemen have long been incentivized to stockpile agricultural supplies, believing that their prices will rise in the event of crop failures and speculation. India's pricing problem has gotten worse as a result of these actions.

Low Industrial Sector Growth: During the early years after independence, in particular, India's industrial sector did not perform up to par. Between 1965 and 1985, it had a dismal 4.7% annual growth rate. Inflation was brought on by lower production and a widening supply-demand differential. Only after 1991 did things start to get better.

Increase in Administered pricing: Coal, steel, electricity, fertilizers, petroleum products, and other commodities had their pricing set by the government. Previously, the government would continuously raise prices in order to bolster the revenue of the ineffective public sector. A rise in the cost of these items impacts the overall level of prices and causes inflation in the economy because the majority of them are used as raw materials for other goods.

## Social Responsibility Of Business

A business's social responsibility pertains to its decisions and actions that prioritize the well-being of society at large in addition to generating profits for the organization. The manner the business firm operates and behaves is intended to achieve both the traditional economic gains that the business firm is interested in and social gains as well. The premise that a corporation has a duty to serve society as it operates inside society and depends on its people and physical resources is the foundation of the concept of social responsibility. The notion that a business that does good deeds for society will ultimately benefit the business itself is also the foundation of the concept of social responsibility.

## Social responsibility towards stakeholders

### Towards owners

Businesses have the following obligations to their owners:

Regularly paying a dividend at a reasonable rate.

Increasing the company's net present value via efficient management.

Ensuring that owners are fully involved in the running of the business.

Providing accurate and thorough reports that include all the details about how the business operates.

Giving out financial data and answering any questions that may have arisen.

## Social responsibility towards stakeholders

### Towards workers

Businesses have the following obligations to their workers:

Employment stability with competitive pay, bonuses, profit-sharing, etc.

Equitable chances for advancement and development within the company.

Training resources and chances for employees to advance their skills.

Promoting company-wide participative management.

Providing improved working conditions, social security, and welfare for employees.

Preserving employees against risks related to their jobs.

Promoting the growth of competent union leadership.

**Towards customers**

Ensuring that goods are available in the appropriate amount, at the appropriate location, and at the appropriate time.

Providing top-notch items.

Maintaining fair rates for its goods.

Employing appropriate metrics.

Offering top-notch post-purchase assistance.

Clear of unfair trade tactics and other techniques that take advantage of customers.

Supporting the establishment of consumer advisory councils and associations and preserving strong ties with them.

Creating suitable goods and services to meet customer demands.

**Social responsibility for economic growth**

Organizations absorb information from the society in which they function. These inputs are transformed into goods or services that are most beneficial to society. Businesses cannot focus exclusively on the maximization of profits. It is essential to take society's economic progress into account. For the economic advancement of society, organizations need to take advantage of all available environmental opportunities. Through new business endeavors, an organization can increase its revenue. Additionally, this results in the creation of new job prospects for the populace. Opportunities for employment raise people's standards of living. The ways that social responsibility supports a developing economy are as follows:

## Best possible use of available resources:

In nature, resources are scarce. An organization is expected to spend resources justly by abiding by its social obligations. Resources must be employed to produce goods and services that do not conflict with the interests of the general public. It is not expected of an organization to generate items that are unneeded or undesirable. In addition to depleting national resources, the production of these commodities encourages individuals to spend money on pointless purchases.

Efficient production of commodities and services that promote societal economic well-being: Organizations are required to generate items with little wastage. Businesses are required to implement business process reengineering. This aids the company in finding fresh and more effective approaches to enhancing the final product. Additionally, product safety is considered. Each of these elements supports the society's economic health.

In addition to maintaining public spaces and keeping traffic and slums out of the way, organizations are required to preserve the environment. It is unable to transfer this obligation to the government. When there is a healthy environment, the organization takes the initiative to keep the surrounding areas free of pollution, traffic, and slums.

**To Whom Are Organisations Socially Responsible?**

A business has a social responsibility to contribute towards the betterment of society. To whom do organizations owe their social responsibility? The shareholders model states that an organization's only social duty is to maximize shareholder wealth through maximizing business profits. The stakeholder model states that businesses are required to meet the demands and interests of several corporate shareholders, not just one. Nonetheless, the organization's key stakeholders' requirements—which are essential to its survival—take precedence over secondary stakeholders' wants.

A company's social duty is largely shaped by its economic and legal obligations rather than its moral and subjective obligations. However, the expectations society has of corporate social responsibility at a given moment determines the relative prominence of economic, legal, ethical, and discretionary duties. One hundred years ago, the expectations of society were primarily for businesses to fulfil their legal and economic obligations. However, ethical and discretionary obligations are now far more significant than they were in the past when society evaluates whether businesses are socially responsible.

In order to fulfil their financial obligations, businesses are expected to uphold the laws and regulations of the society in which they operate. This is known as legal responsibility. For instance, it is currently unlawful to sell freshly baked bread in the USA due to the Clean Air Act of 1990. The ethanol released during the baking of bread is what makes it illegal, not the scent. Although ethanol is not poisonous in and of itself, it does add to pollution because it encourages the production of ozone, a dangerous atmospheric gas. Large baking facilities may therefore need to invest millions on catalytic oxidizers—which eliminate ethanol emissions—in order to comply with the law.

The obligation placed on organisations by society to conduct business in a way that upholds established moral and ethical standards is known as their ethical responsibility. Satisfying ethical responsibilities is more challenging than satisfying economic or legal commitments since diverse stakeholders may disagree about what constitutes an ethical behaviour.

Beyond their obligations to the economy, law, and ethics, businesses also have discretionary responsibilities to society. It is optional to exercise discretion. If they do not carry them out, businesses will not be regarded as unethical.

### Corporate Social Reporting: Major heads

(i) Opportunities in India and opportunities elsewhere can be used to categories the creation of employment chances throughout the year. In India, jobs can be generated by diversification or development into underdeveloped or other areas. On the other hand, job prospects may also be regarded as employment protection through the absorption of ill units. Furthermore, by taking on foreign initiatives, the corporate entity can open up new opportunities overseas. Quantitative data that breaks down the number of SC/ST individuals, physically disabled individuals, women, and other employees hired over the course of the year must be provided in all such circumstances. It's important to fully disclose any tax benefits or subsidies obtained for building industrial facilities in underdeveloped areas or absorbing ill facilities.

(ii) It is preferable to reveal foreign exchange transactions in full, especially considering the little foreign exchange reserve. Exports and proceeds from overseas projects are the sources of foreign exchange inflows. Additionally, foreign exchange inflows and savings are equal. By substituting foreign technology and technicians with imports and replacing foreign exchange with imports, an organisation can save foreign exchange. Purchases of raw materials and/or replacement parts, capital repayment for plants and machines, dividend payments, and interest payments are the main causes of foreign exchange outflows. Reporting the inflows statement in Indian rupees is preferable. Any tax benefit or export subsidy obtained in exchange for foreign exchange profits must be declared as a societal cost.

(iii) Research and development expenses, whether recurring or non-requiring, must be published together with the findings. Research and development efforts can potentially be measured in terms of profit added or cost savings. Any tax gain or subsidy obtained must be declared as a social cost in addition to any social advantages that result from research and development.,

(iv) It is necessary to disclose as a social benefit any money paid to the government exchequer through sales tax, income tax, excise, customs, and other levies.

(v) The contribution of social projects can be further divided into donations to various organizations and the active involvement of business enterprise. Social projects like building a road, establishing a school, college, hospital, stadium, etc., can be designated with the costs and beneficiary groups.

When donating to any kind of organization, it is possible to specify the type of organization as well as the benefits derived from the donation.

(The business enterprise's contribution to the advancement of games, sports, cultural issues, and self-employment initiatives may be documented as the creation of social benefit.).

## CSR Provisions in Companies Act, 2013

### Section 135: Corporate Social Responsibility

This provision aims to establish that the Corporate Social Responsibility Committee of the Board shall consist of all companies with a certain net worth, sales, or net profit during any given financial year. The Board's Report will list the committee's membership. The Committee is responsible for creating policy, which will include the tasks listed in Schedule VII. It further states that the Board will make sure that each year, at least two percent of the company's average net income from the three financial years that came before would be allocated to this kind of policy. In the event that the company is unable to spend this amount, the Board will explain why in its report.

Incorporated into a business model, corporate social responsibility (CSR) is a type of self-regulation. It is sometimes referred to as social performance, corporate citizenship, sustainable business, or responsible business.

Internal and external stakeholders are involved in CSR. The government and shareholders are examples of internal stakeholders. To be implemented successfully, corporate social responsibility must have strong leadership. The development of the next generation of globally responsible leaders is therefore imperative, and leadership plays a critical role in all CSR initiatives.

### Application of Provision

A CSR Committee of Board consisting of three or more directors, one of whom must be an independent director, must be formed by companies with a net value of at least Rs. 500 crores, a turnover of at least Rs. 1,000 crores, or a net profit of at least Rs. 5 crores during any given financial year.

### Composition of CSR Committee

Eligible companies must constitute a CSR Committee comprising at least three directors, including at least one independent director. For unlisted public and private companies that are not required to appoint independent directors, the CSR Committee can consist of two directors.

There must be three or more directors on the CSR committee, with one of them being an independent. As mandated by Section 134(4), the composition of the Corporate Social Responsibility Committee must be revealed in the Board's Report.

A private firm or an unlisted public company that is exempt from the requirement to choose an independent director must have an independent director on its CSR Committee.

A private firm with just two members on its board will appoint two of those directors to serve on its CSR committee.

The CSR Committee for a foreign firm must consist of a minimum of two individuals: one must be an Indian resident and the other must be a nominee of the foreign company.

Eligible companies must constitute a CSR Committee comprising at least three directors, including at least one independent director. For unlisted public and private companies that are not required to appoint independent directors, the CSR Committee can consist of two directors.

## CSR Activities

The Companies Act of 2013 does not specify the process that a corporation must follow in order to carry out CSR initiatives. Businesses now have the freedom to select programmes, decide which activities to do within the framework, carry them out however they see fit, monitor them, and make sure their own CSR policies are being followed. Nonetheless, the following approaches may be used to carry out the CSR activities:

By Charity: Businesses can give money to a range of trusts, societies, NGOs, and other charitable organizations that support the social and economic welfare of society.

By Contract: The firm may appoint an NGO or similar organization to handle initiatives on its behalf.

A Corporate Social Responsibility Policy (CSRP), which outlines the actions the firm must take in accordance with Schedule VII of the Act, must be developed by the CSRC and recommended to the Board. The Committee will suggest how much money should be spent on these initiatives. The Committee will also occasionally check in on the company's CSR policy.

The Board will post the CSR Policy on the corporate website, if one exists, and reveal its contents in its report, as approved by the Board based on the suggestions given by the CSR Committee.

The following CSR actions that the corporation is required to carry out are outlined in Schedule VII and are explained below:

Eliminating poverty, hunger, and malnutrition; supplying clean, safe drinking water; and offering preventive healthcare and sanitation;

Encouraging livelihood improvement initiatives, special education, and career-enhancing skills for work, particularly among women, children, the elderly, and those with disabilities;

Encouraging gender parity, empowering women, establishing orphanages and home for them, as well as senior citizen amenities such daycare centres and old age homes, as well as steps to lessen the disparities that socially and economically disadvantaged groups must contend with;

Sustaining the sustainability of the environment, ecological balance, animal welfare, flora and wildlife protection, agroforestry, natural resource conservation, and soil, air, and water quality;

Preservation of the nation's artistic and cultural legacy, including the preservation of historical buildings, landmarks, and artwork; establishment of public libraries; encouragement of the growth of traditional handicrafts and arts; Policies to support veterans of the armed forces, widows of war, and their dependents;

Instruction in rural sports, national sports, Olympic sports, and paralympic sports;

Donation to the Prime Minister's National Relief Fund or any other fund established by the federal government or state governments for the purpose of promoting socioeconomic development, providing aid, and ensuring the welfare of women, minorities, and other underprivileged groups as well as Scheduled Castes and Scheduled Tribes.

## Role of the Board

The Board of every company shall –

The Board to compose a Corporate Social Responsibility Committee.

Following receipt of the Corporate Social Responsibility Committee's recommendation and policy, approve and carry out the company's CSR policy. This includes disclosing the policy in the Board's Report in accordance with Section 134, Subsection (3), for a fiscal year that begins on or after April 1, 2014, and posting the policy's contents on the company's website, if applicable, in the format required by the Companies (Corporate Social Responsibility Policy) Rules, 2014. The Board makes sure that the company properly carries out the initiatives that the CSR Committee formulated for the Policy.

In line with its Corporate Social Responsibility Policy, the Board makes sure that the company spends, in each fiscal year, a minimum of two percent of its average net profits—which are determined in compliance with Section 198—that it made in the three fiscal years prior. When allocating funds for Corporate Social Responsibility (CSR) activities, the company will prioritise the local community and surrounding areas in which it works, in accordance with the CSR Policy.

## Penalty

In accordance with Clause (o) of sub-section (3) of section 134, the Board must declare and provide a justification in its report if the firm does not spend the required amount, which is equivalent to at least two percent of the average net profit.

According to Section 134 of the Companies Act of 2013, failure on the part of the Company to disclose such information will result in a fine that may not be less than fifty thousand rupees but may reach twenty-five lakh rupees. Additionally, any officer of the Company who fails to comply will face imprisonment for a maximum term of three years or a fine that may not be less than fifty thousand rupees but may reach five lakh rupees.

## Internal Environment

A precise evaluation internal analysis of the organization, and a clear definition of the mission of the business are the cornerstones of every effective and efficient strategy. For the organization to succeed, at least three components are needed. They are mentioned as follows:

The competitive environment's conditions must be accommodated by the strategy. The organization's or company's internal resources and capabilities must be realistically required by the strategy, which also needs to be carefully developed, implemented, controlled, and carried out.

For the strategist, doing an inside examination of the company is a highly tough and demanding assignment. It is possible to create a realistic company profile through internal study. In addition to objective and systematic analysis, it frequently incorporates trade-offs, value system judgments, educated guesswork, and expertise. An organized internal analysis leads to the organization profile's primary goal. Creating a realistic mission and a strategy are crucial for achieving the goals of the plan.

Organizational strategy-based internal analysis must pinpoint the organization's opportunities, weaknesses, threats, and strengths. Organizational analysis determines a SWOT-based appropriate approach. Value systems, mission objectives, management structure and nature, integrated power relationships, human resources, company/organization image and brand equity, physical assets, aspects of research and development (R&D), technological capabilities, marketing resources, and financial resource factors are just a few examples of the important internal factors that can be identified and evaluated in the first step of internal analysis.

## External Environment

### Suppliers

Suppliers provide raw material supply to the companies. Due to supply limits or supply uncertainty, businesses are frequently forced to keep large inventories, which raises costs. It had been noted that, in contrast to Japan, where inventories typically held inventory for a few hours to two weeks, Indian industries kept 3–4 months of local and 9 months of imported supplies. But the situation has changed significantly as a result of the liberalization.

Due to the supply's sensitivity, a lot of businesses place a great value on vendor development. When possible, vertical integration aids in resolving the supply issue. Nirma, for instance, has long supported the idea that the best approach to control manufacturing costs is to establish captive production facilities for raw materials, and it has embraced a massive backward integration.

However, outsourcing often proves to be more advantageous. Dependence on a single supplier carries a high risk because any production issue, such as a lockout or strike, could have a major negative impact on the business. Likewise, alterations in the supplier's demeanour or outlook could potentially impact the organisation. Therefore, having a variety of supply sources can help lower these risks.

## Customers

A company's competitors are all those that vie for customers' discretionary cash in addition to other businesses that sell same or comparable goods. For instance, companies that sell televisions may face competition from other TV manufacturers as well as from businesses that sell two-wheelers, refrigerators, cooking ranges, stereo sets, and other products, as well as from organizations that offer savings and investment plans such as banks, Unit Trust of India, businesses that take deposits from the general public, and businesses that issue shares or debentures, among others. Since the main objective is to impact the consumer's fundamental want, this competition between various products may be referred to as a desire competition. Desire competition is typically highly high in countries with limited disposable incomes, lots of unfulfilled needs, and lots of options for how to spend and invest the disposable income.

The consumer will still have a lot of options to select from, including TV, stereo, two-in-one, three-in-one, and so on, if he chooses to spend his discretionary cash on recreation (or recreation cum education). Generic competition refers to the competition between such alternatives that fulfil a specific type of desire.

## Marketing Intermediaries

The marketing intermediaries comprise middlemen like merchants and agents who assist the company in finding customers or closing sales with them. Physical distribution companies like warehouses and transportation companies assist the company in stocking and moving goods from their origin to their destination. Marketing service providers assist the company in targeting and promoting its products to the right markets.

Intermediaries in marketing are essential connections between the business and the end users. A broken or disrupted link, or an incorrect link selection, could have severe consequences for the business. India's retail chemists and chemists once made the decision to boycott a major company's products due to a problem like a low retail margin. The MRTP Commission, however, opposed this collective boycott initiative; had this been accepted, the corporation might have faced legal repercussions. Hindustan Lever also had a significant obstacle when a concerted boycott over trade margin was launched in Kerala.

## Financiers and Banks

The company's financiers are a significant additional micro environmental component. In addition to their financial resources, other critical factors include their policies and strategies, attitudes—including how they view risk—and their capacity to offer non-financial support.

## Environment of Business

## Economic environment

The economic environment is made up of the economic policies, conditions, and system that are significant to the external business elements. The nation's economic circumstances include:

Character of the national economy. The overall state of the economy in the area, the state of the money and material markets, the supply markets, raw material components, services, and so forth all have an impact on how the organization receives inputs, including their costs and the dependability, quality, and availability of the goods and services supplied.

It establishes the market's economic strength and weakness. An individual's purchasing power is influenced by a number of economic factors, including price, savings, debt, availability of credit, and money circulation.

The income distribution pattern of individuals examines market opportunities and their effects on businesses. The nation's development process; the availability of its economic resources; the amount of its economic income; and the distribution of wealth and income.

## Politico legal environment

The political environment encompasses the governmental and legal domains. It is closely related to both economic policy and the economic system. For example, the economies of the communist nations were centrally planned. Laws in nations with communist governments regulate investments and related issues. Numerous laws govern how businesses must conduct themselves. These rules address things like corporate output and service standards.

The parliament of a democratic nation passes laws and other acts. Next, in accordance with the legislation, there are regulatory norms and corporate regulation.

Political stability, accountability, morality and ideology in politics, state of law and order, the ruling party's policies, and the general efficacy and purpose of government agencies are all important factors.

The political and legal environment is made up of the following three crucial components:

## Government

The state's commercial companies and their operations are governed and overseen by government policies, rules, and regulations. Second, what is the state's business policy and how is it administered by the government? The strategist should assess these items from a business perspective. A strategist should research the effects on the business of changes to the government's regulatory framework. Government tax laws are important and have an impact on state commercial organizations.

## Legal

A strong legal framework is a prerequisite for conducting business in the state. A strategist needs to be knowledgeable of the several business rules that safeguard their company, rivals, and customers. Businesses need to be aware of the rules that apply to them, their rivals, intellectual property, foreign exchange, labour, and other matters.

## Political

The political system has an impact on business and its operations as well.

Political pressure groups have an impact on the government, which helps to control and regulate corporate activity nationally.

Political action committees and special interest groups have recently exerted pressure on commercial organizations to give women's, minority, and consumer rights greater consideration.

Aside from the occasional protests against certain goods and services as well as certain state-run businesses.

## Socio cultural environment

The sociocultural environment is a crucial component that needs to be considered while developing corporate business strategies. A company's business is impacted if it disregards its employees' education, tastes, traditions, and conventions. It is made up of elements that have to do with interpersonal relationships as well as the effects of cultural values and societal attitudes. These have an impact on the organization's operations. Effective use of socio-cultural contextual aspects and proper techniques are key components of successful business organizations. An essential component for MNCs is the social and cultural environment. As a result, MNC ought to research the social and cultural landscape of the area in which they are setting up shop. Even when people from different cultural backgrounds use the same basic product, their modes of consumption, conditions under which they use it, or their perceptions of its attributes may differ to the point where different market segments require different approaches to product promotion and attribute presentation.

The following are some examples of how sociocultural elements affect an organization's working environment:

Social concerns include the place of business in society, pollution of the environment, corruption, the use of the media, and the use of the company's goods and services.

Society expects businesses to address social attitude and value issues such as materialism, shifting lifestyle patterns, and social norms, beliefs, rituals, and practices.

The functioning of company is also impacted by changes in family structure, values, and attitudes.

The place, role, and nature of duties that women have in society have an impact on business and how it operates in the marketplace.

The functioning of business can be influenced by factors such as educational attainment, societal awareness and consciousness of rights, and work ethics.

Social practices, beliefs, and related elements are useful for promoting specific goods, services, or ideas; the success of marketing is largely dependent on how well social attitudes or value systems are changed.

**Natural environment**

Natural environment studies focuses on a significant aspect of the natural world, the natural environment. Geographical and ecological elements are included in the natural environment as follows:

Endowments in natural resources;

Weather; climate; and topographical considerations

Location factors in a global perspective

Industries that support the material index are also influenced by geographic and ecological considerations, and they are typically found close to the sources of raw materials. The location of some sectors, like the textile industry, is influenced by the climate and weather.

Recently, ecological factors have grown in significance.

Natural resource depletion, contamination of the environment, and disruption of the ecological balance have all raised serious concerns. Government policies intended to preserve the environment and maintain an ecological balance, as well as to conserve non-replenishable resources, have left businesses with new obligations and challenges. Some of these have increased the cost of production and marketing, and externalities have emerged as a significant issue that businesses must deal with.

## Technological environment

Technology can occasionally cause major issues. A company might not survive if it cannot adapt to technological developments. Furthermore, product alterations may be necessary due to the varying technology environments of different markets or nations. The most significant component of the macro environment is technology. Technology is genuinely amazing and represents human ingenuity. Technological developments have made it easier to introduce new items and enhance existing ones, thus increasing their marketability. Businesses have also faced difficulties as a result of the rapid changes in technology, which are making plants and products outdated. Adopting modern technological advancements is essential for success in business and industry.

A component of global technical progress is the internet and telecom infrastructure. The world was altered by these events of today. People and company operations are altered by it. In addition to the numerous current systems, it opens up a plethora of new business prospects. Here are some aspects of the technological environment:

## Types of Economic Systems

## Economy of Free Enterprise

The foundation of this economic system is the Laissez Faire concept, which calls for the least amount of intervention from the state or other outside forces. If the government has any role at all, it is primarily responsible for ensuring that the economy operates freely by removing barriers to unrestricted competition.

The following traits of a free enterprise economy are present:

The primary driving force behind economic activity is private gain. Consumers and firms both enjoy freedom of choice, allowing them to consume or produce as they please. Factor owners also enjoy freedom of occupational choice, allowing them to use their resources in any lawful business or occupation. Finally, there is intense competition in both commodity and factor markets.

The government tries to keep its traditional tasks, such as defence, law enforcement, justice, certain financial institutions, and public utility services, to a minimum; it should not meddle in people's economic affairs.

## Economy under Government Control

The terms "command," "centrally planned," or "socialist" also apply to economies under government control. These economies are managed, regulated, and under the authority of government agencies, as opposed to free enterprise economies.

Other characteristics of a strictly socialist economy include:

The means of production are owned by the state or society in the name of the community; private ownership of factors and property is abolished; the economy is guided by social welfare rather than by personal gain, motivation, or initiative; consumer choice is limited to what society can afford for all; and the role of competition and market forces is eliminated by law.

## Mixed Economy

An economy that combines both the public and private sectors is known as a mixed economy. It aims to bring together the best aspects of socialism and free market economies. An economy that consists of both the "public sector," or the government economy, and the "private sector," or the private economy, is referred to as a mixed economy. There are elements of a socialist economy in the public sector and a free market economy in the private sector. The majority of economies in the world today are mixed economies, it is crucial to remember this.

Mixed Economies come in two different varieties.

Diverse Capitalist Systems
One variation of the free enterprise economic system is the mixed capitalist economy.

Highly developed countries like the United States, the United Kingdom, France, Japan, and others fall into this group. Despite having sizable public sectors, their private sectors operate according to the free enterprise system. The government is crucial in maintaining the capitalist mode of production, guaranteeing competitiveness in the markets for factors and products, and supplying the means to support economic activity in the private sector 19.

Societies with Mixed Economies
The countries that have adopted the "socialist pattern of society: and economic planning as he means of growth and social justice" (like India) and the former communist nations (like China and Russia) that have recently implemented drastic economic reforms and liberalised their economies for private entrepreneurship fall into the

category of mixed socialist economies. The governments of these nations assume the responsibility of overseeing and regulating the operations of the private sector in compliance with the goals of the plans.

## Essential economic problems and the purpose of government

Regardless of the structure of the economic system, all economies have encountered a few fundamental issues. The main economic issues that confront an economy can be divided into two main categories: (i) basic problems, or micro-economic issues, which deal with how the economic system's constituents function; and (ii) macro-economic issues, which deal with the expansion, stability, and management of the economy as a whole.

The nature of an economy determines how its fundamental issues are resolved. In a mixed capitalism or free business economy, the Price Mechanism or Market Mechanism handles these problems, whereas in a socialist economy the government institutions, such as the Central Planning Authority, handle them.

Even while a free enterprise system can lead to economic progress, it cannot guarantee steady, balanced growth. Thus, it becomes necessary for the government to step in and promote fair competition in order to assist the economy in reaching its objectives of efficiency, stability, growth, and economic fairness.

The question now becomes what shape, what kind, and how much the government should interfere in the workings of the market, or what role the government should play in managing the nation's economy.

However, the three dominant economic systems in the world today—the capitalist system, also known as the free enterprise system, the socialist system, and the mixed economy system-allow for a general classification of the government's economic function.

The Capital Society Under this system, the government's main responsibilities are to: (i) protect and enhance free market mechanisms wherever possible to guarantee a competitive market that works; (ii) remove any unnecessary barriers to the free operation of a market that is competitive; and (iii) provide the market with the necessary playground and rules through necessary interventions and controls to enable free competition to function.

It can be deduced that in a capitalist society, the government's role is limited to two things: (a) restoring and promoting the conditions required for the free market mechanism to function efficiently, and (b) entering the production and distribution sectors where private entrepreneurship is either absent or ineffective.

Socialist Economy: In accordance with the capitalist system, a socialist economy places a far greater emphasis on the function of the state. In the former, the government was only allowed to have a limited involvement in the economy; in the later, however, it has complete authority over nearly all economic activity. Not only are market mechanisms and free entrepreneurship completely disregarded in the socialist system, but these systems are actually outlawed.

The state acquires ownership of the factors of production, replacing private ownership. The State plans, directs, and controls all economic activity centrally. All decisions pertaining to pricing, employment, resource allocation, and production are made centrally by the government or the Central Planning Authority.

Mixed Economy: In this system, the private sector, which makes up a large portion of the economy, is permitted to operate under the tenets of the free market or free enterprise system within a wide range of political and economic policy guidelines.

The public sector, which makes up the other half of the economy, is set up and run in a socialist manner. By designating specific businesses, trades, services, and activities for government oversight and control, the public sector is established. By means of an ordinance, the government forbids the introduction of private capital into businesses designated for the public sector. Nationalization of current industries is an additional means of establishing or growing the public sector. The State alone bears the duty for the development, supervision, and administration of the public sector industries.

Through its industrial, monetary, and fiscal policies, the government supervises and controls the private sector in addition to overseeing and administering the public sector industries. Direct controls are also implemented if needed.

## Case Study 1

Amal was a talented person being trained for a role as Controller at a mid-sized manufacturing company. Following his first year as an assistant controller, the firm's officers began to include him in important business operations. For example, he was at a famous consulting firm today for the monthly financial statement summary. Amal found it fascinating during the discussion how the consultant turned all the financial data he had been gathering into informative charts and graphs.

Up until the consultant began discussing the new production plant the company was adding to the current location and the costs per unit of the chemically plated products it produced, Amal was generally enthusiastic about the session and the future of the company. Gopal, the chemical engineer, and Vishnu, the president, began discussing issues related to waste treatment and disposal at that point. Although they may still meet federal requirements, Gopal stated that the current waste facilities were unable to handle the waste materials that would be produced by the "ultramodern" new facility in a way that would meet the industry's pretty high standards.

For the remainder of the meeting, Amal did not hear anything. He couldn't stop thinking how the business could be so careless about the environment. However, he was unsure of when, how, or even if he could express his viewpoint. He soon began to consider if this was the proper firm for him.

What are the relevant facts?

What are the ethical issues?

What are the practical constraints?

**Case Study 2**

Joe recently received a promotion to the role of District Manager for Computer Operations at a major corporation. Joe's manager, Mary, summons him to her workspace. She recently learned that an anonymous letter from an employee was sent to the CEO. This letter reports that a highly expensive system that was just built does not operate as planned or provide the desired outcomes. Joe is aware that the anonymous letter accurately describes the system's actual functioning. Joe had already told Mary about this performance issue. Despite having listened to Joe, Mary was the one who initially endorsed the system and consistently gives the CEO constructive criticism regarding its operation.

Mary informs Joe that a response to the letter is anticipated by the CEO. Joe is told to prepare the response by her. It should state that all of the savings indicated in the initial justification documents are being realised and that the system is operating as anticipated. She argues those claims should be backed up by the material he included with his response. He comes up to Mary and expresses his worry. She says she will seriously doubt his capacity to carry out the duties of a District Manager for the organisation if he does not respond to her request. Joe is rather concerned because he has worked hard to get this position.

What are the relevant facts?

What are the ethical issues?

What actions should be taken?

## Questions

| Question | Option 1 | Option 2 | Option 3 | Option 4 | Answer |
|---|---|---|---|---|---|
| Indicate the nature of Indian Economy | Capitalist economy | Closed economy | Mixed Economy | None of these | 3 |
| Predict the economy that is free from any government intervention | Closed Economy | Mixed Economy | Free market economy | None of these | 3 |
| Predict the outlook of Indian plans | Economic Growth | Industrial expansion | Growth with social justice | None of these | 3 |
| Predict the outlook of Indian plans | Economic Growth | Industrial expansion | Growth with social justice | None of these | 3 |
| Indicate the policy of govt. related to Export and Import | IMEX policy | EXIM policy | Export policy | None of these | 2 |

| Predict the full form of SEZ | Special Economic Zone | Special Export Zone | Socially Backward Zone | None of these | 1 |
| Identify the environment that consist of economic condition, economic policies, industrial policies and economic system | Business environment | Economic Environment | Natural Environment | None of these | 2 |
| Identify the nature of PESTLE as an analytical tool | An internal analysis | An external analysis | A competitor analysis | A strategic analysis | 4 |
| Select the tools of the external environment those are uncontrollable and | Strengths and opportunities | Strength and weakness | Weakness and threats | Opportunities and threats | 4 |

| | | | | | |
|---|---|---|---|---|---|
| external to business | | | | | |
| Infer the type of economic system, the Govt. intervention is maximum | Free enterprise economy | Socialist economy | Mixed economy | None of these | 1 |
| Infer the economic system where the means of production are owned and managed by the jointly by State and private organizations | Capitalism | Socialism | Mixed Economy | Common economy | 3 |
| Select the economic system that is known as 'Laissez faire' | Social | Capitalist | Mixed | None of these | 2 |

| Predict the process of the sale of sub-standard and hazardous goods under defined conditions | Restrictive Trade Practice | Unfair Trade Practice | MRTP | None of these | 2 |
|---|---|---|---|---|---|
| Indicate the external force which have direct effect on the functioning of the business | Environment | Culture | System | None of these | 1 |
| Predict the force in the company's immediate environment that affect the performance of the Co | Macro environment | Micro environment | Technological environment | Natural environment | 2 |

| | | | | | |
|---|---|---|---|---|---|
| Select the type of economic system, where the Govt. intervention is absent. | Free enterprise economy | Socialist economy | Mixed economy | Natural environment | 1 |
| Select the economic system where the means of production are owned and managed by the State | Capitalism | Socialism | Mixed Economy | Common economy | 2 |
| Indicate the economic system where both private and public sector exists | Social | Capitalist | Mixed | Common economy | 3 |

| |
|---|
| Explain the factors influencing corporate governance. |
| Explain importance of social responsibility of business. |
| Explain characteristics of multi-national corporations. |
| Describe National Income equation in closed economy. |
| Describe different types of unemployment. |
| Describe role of Government of India in eradication of poverty and unemployment. |
| Describe National Income equation in open economy. |
| Discuss for and against liberal economy. |
| Discuss for and against socialism. |
| Discuss for and against capitalism. |
| Discuss for and against mixed economy. |
| Discuss success of India as mixed economy |
| Explain causes of poverty. |
| Explain causes of unemployment. |
| Explain effects of infrastructure development in an economy. |
| Explain for and against planning. |

# Chapter - 2
# Macroeconomic Variables

**CHAPTER CONTENT**

National Income

Monetary Policy

Fiscal Policy

Industrial Policy

## National Income:

### Meaning and Definition

A nation's economic well-being is solely determined by the quantity of products and services it provides to meet its citizens' consumption demands. The national income of a nation can be a useful indicator of its economic welfare. The flow of products and services that become accessible to a nation in a given year is known as national income. National Income is therefore a flow rather than a stock.

The total monetary worth of all products and services generated in a given year, less deductions for wear and tear and the depreciation of equipment and plants utilized in the production of goods and services, is known as national income. It is the monetary equivalent, or value, of the net total goods and services that a country has access to each year as a result of the economic activity of the community as a whole, which includes social and political institutions, businesses, and homes and individuals.

## National Income: Key concepts

### 1  Gross Domestic Product (GDP)

**Definition:** The total monetary value of all final goods and services produced within a country's borders in a specific time period.

### Types:

**Nominal GDP:** Measured at current market prices without adjusting for inflation.

**Real GDP:** Adjusted for inflation, providing a more accurate reflection of an economy's size and how it's growing over time.

### 2  Gross National Product (GNP):

**Definition:** The total value of all final goods and services produced by the residents of a country in a specific time period, including those produced abroad.

**Formula:** GNP = GDP + Net Income from Abroad (income earned by residents from overseas investments minus income earned by foreigners within the country).

### 3  Net National Product (NNP):

**Definition:** GNP minus depreciation (the value of wear and tear on the country's capital goods).

**Formula:** NNP = GNP - Depreciation.

## 4 National Income (NI)

**Definition:** The total income earned by a nation's residents in the production of goods and services.

**Formula:** NI = NNP - Indirect Taxes + Subsidies.

## 5 Personal Income (PI)

**Definition:** The total income received by individuals and households in a country, including wages, salaries, and transfer payments (e.g., social security, unemployment benefits).

**Formula:** PI = NI - Corporate Taxes - Retained Earnings + Transfer Payments.

## 6 Disposable Personal Income (DPI)

**Definition:** The amount of money that households have available for spending and saving after income taxes have been accounted for.

**Formula:** DPI = PI - Personal Taxes.

Methods of Calculating National Income

## 1 Production (Output) Method

Measures the value of output produced by each of the major sectors of the economy: agriculture, industry, and services.

GDP (by production) = Sum of Value Added by all sectors.

## 2. Income Method:

Measures the total income earned by the factors of production within the economy: wages, rent, interest, and profit.

GDP (by income) = Wages + Rent + Interest + Profit.

## 3. Expenditure Method

Measures the total spending on the final goods and services produced within a country.

GDP (by expenditure) = Consumption + Investment + Government Spending + (Exports - Imports).

## Importance of National Income Statistics

1. **Economic Performance:** Indicates the overall economic health and growth rate of a country.

2. **Policy Formulation:** Helps governments in making informed economic policies and decisions.

3. **Comparative Analysis:** Facilitates comparison of economic performance across different countries and regions.

4. **Standard of Living:** Provides insights into the standard of living and economic well-being of the population.

5. **Investment Decisions:** Assists investors in making decisions based on economic conditions.

## Challenges in Measuring National Income

1. **Informal Economy:** Difficulty in capturing data from unorganized sectors and informal economy.

2. **Data Accuracy:** Ensuring accurate and timely data collection.

3. **Non-Market Transactions:** Exclusion of household work and volunteer services that do not have market prices.

4. **Environmental Costs:** GDP does not account for environmental degradation and resource depletion.

5. **Income Distribution:** National income figures may not reflect income inequalities within a country.

## Monetary Policy

The term "monetary policy" refers to a regulatory strategy whereby the central bank keeps control over the money supply in order to achieve overall economic objectives.

"Policy employing the Central bank's control of the money supply as an instrument for achieving the objectives of general economic policies" is how H.G. Johnson describes monetary policy.

Therefore, the term "monetary policy" refers to actions intended to influence the availability, cost, and supply of money in order to guarantee the economic system operates more effectively. It entails the purposeful use of monetary instruments to achieve economic policy goals.

The Bank Rate, Open Market Operations, and Variable Reserve Requirements are the three broad or quantitative instruments of credit regulation and monetary policy.

It is crucial to emphasize that the general credit control techniques are interdependent and require collaboration while examining them. The amount of bank reserves is impacted by each of the three instruments. The reserve base is directly impacted by open market operations and reserve requirements, but the bank rate has an indirect effect due to changes in the cost of obtaining reserves.

Which tool is used instead of another at any given time depends on the circumstances, the extent of the desired influence, and how quickly the change needs to be implemented. For example, Open Market Operations can handle daily adjustments on even the smallest scale. Reserve requirement changes have an instantaneous effect on the banks as a whole. Changes in bank rates have an impact on the banking system and the short-term money market, but they also have broader implications on the economy overall.

Bank Rate Guidelines: The oldest tool used in monetary policy is the Bank Rate, sometimes referred to as the Discount Rate. According to conventional wisdom, the bank rate is the amount that the central bank deducts from, or rather, rediscounts, qualifying invoices. Nowadays, though, the word "bank rate" has a broader definition and describes the lowest interest rate at which the central bank offers financial support to commercial banks in order to fulfil its role as the lender of last resort.

The interest rate that the central bank charges on advances it makes to commercial banks will rise in response to an increase in the bank rate. Therefore, a rise in the Bank Rate forces commercial banks to raise the interest rates on the loans and advances they provide to their clients, and vice versa.

The Bank Rate sets the standard for all other interest rates, which makes it extremely significant. A change in the Discount rate is immediately and efficiently reflected in all market rates in a well-established money market, such as the London Money Market.

Open Market Operations: In general, open market operations relate to the Central Bank's buying and selling of a range of assets, including gold, foreign exchange, government securities, and even corporate shares. In actuality, though, they are limited to the buying and selling of government assets in India.

Through Open Market Operations, the central bank aims to impact the economy by either expanding or contracting the money supply.

The central bank purchases securities from the public and commercial banks in order to expand the money supply. For example, in the first instance, the reserves of commercial banks and public currency will rise by around 100 crore if the Reserve Bank of India purchases assets valued at 100 crore. The final growth in the money supply, though, may be far more.

The rise in reserves that occurs when the central bank buys securities from commercial banks may lead to the development of multiple credit. Sometimes, if the sellers of securities deposit the receipts with commercial banks, the public purchase could result in an extension of credit and an increase in the banking system's reserves. The opposite results occur when the central bank sells securities.

The Reserve Bank has used open market operations largely to support government borrowing initiatives and to keep the gilt-edged market in an orderly manner. This instrument has been employed in this process to groom the market by buying securities that are about to mature in order to enable redemption and by making a range of loans available on tap in order to expand the gilt-edged market. As the government's banker, the Reserve Bank has a responsibility to establish gilt-edged market conditions that support the borrowing and refunding activities of the government. However, the way the government arranges its credit programmes is harmonious with the overall stability of the capital and money markets. Banks have also benefited from seasonal financing provided by open market operations. In order to increase credit to business and industry during the slow season, banks often invest their excess cash in government securities, which they then sell (or borrow against) during the busy season. The Reserve Bank is typically prepared to deal in these securities.

Variable Reserve Ratio: Every nation's commercial banks are required by law or custom to retain a specific portion of their deposits as balances with the central bank. This reserve requirement may be changed by the central bank, and changes to reserve requirements have an impact on commercial banks' ability to provide credit. In the event that the reserve requirement is set at 10%, the bank's maximum loan amount would be equal to 90% of its total reserves. The bank is not permitted to lend more than **80%** of total reserves if the reserve ratio is increased to 20%.

The cash reserve ratio may be changed by the Reserve Bank of India from 3% to 15% of the total demand and time liabilities. With the caveat that the total reserve to be maintained with the Bank should not exceed 15% of their demand and time liabilities, the RBI has also been given the authority to require the scheduled banks to maintain additional cash reserves with it. These reserves will be calculated based on the excess of the scheduled banks' total demand and time liabilities over the level of those liabilities on the base date that the Reserve Bank will notify.

The Reserve Bank of India reduced the CRR to 7.5 percent in March 2001, which was projected to boost the GDP by more than 4000 crore. This illustrates how changes in the CRR can affect the money supply and the overall state of the economy.

Statutory Liquidity Ratio (SLR): Additionally, steps have been taken to stop banks from selling their holdings of government securities in order to counteract the effects of changing reserve requirements.

With the amendment of the Banking Regulation Act, all banks in India are now required to maintain a minimum level of liquid assets, which cannot fall below a predetermined percentage of their demand and time liabilities. This requirement applies only to cash balances that are maintained under Section 42 of the Reserve Bank of India Act for schedule banks and Section 18 of the Banking Regulation Act for non-scheduled banks.

## Money supply in any economy

The aggregate money supply in the nation comes from five sources (M3):

1) The bank's net bank credit
2) Bank financing for the business sector
3) Bank sector's net foreign exchange assets
4) Public currency liabilities of the government
5) Banking sector non-monetary liabilities.

Net Government Bank Credit: The Central and State governments can receive bank credits from RBI or from other banks. These are the two different forms of bank credits to the government. In exchange for loans from the RBI, the government gives the RBI its securities and IOUs. Alongside government securities, the RBI prints and distributes currency notes. As a result, the nation's money supply rises, and it falls when the government buys back its holdings. In a similar vein, borrowing by the government from commercial banks expands the public money supply.

Bank Credit to the Commercial Sector: Banks enhance the amount of money in the public's hands when they lend to their customers. There is a multiplier effect when the commercial sector lends money. When a bank lends money to a consumer, they don't actually give him cash; instead, they give him the option to take out checks. The bank receives these checks back as new deposits. Banks increase their deposits by making more of these loans. Increased bank loans equate to increased money supply and investment.

Foreign Exchange Assets: Notes are a source of money supply and one of the foreign exchange assets that the banking sector has acquired. Upon receiving payment in foreign exchange, or forex, an exporter turns it over to the bank, which then issues him domestic money. As a result, there is more money available in the nation. However, when an importer pays local currency to the bank in order to get foreign exchange for imports, the amount of money in the nation decreases.

Public Liabilities in Government Currency: The Indian government issues currency to the general people in the form of one-rupee notes, rupee coins, and tiny coins. As a result, there is an increase in the amount of money in circulation and in the public debt held by the government.

### India's monetary policy

The Chakravarthy Committee has highlighted that the key goals of monetary policy in India have been price stability, growth, equity and social justice, as well as the encouragement and development of new financial institutions. Since 1952, the government's monetary policy has placed a strong emphasis on the two main goals of its economic policy: a. accelerating the nation's economic development to enhance national income and quality of living; and b. controlling and reducing inflationary pressures in the economy.

The Reserve Bank of India develops and implements the country's monetary policy in order to accomplish particular goals. It refers to the strategy used by the nation's central bank to regulate

(i) The money supply and

(ii) The interest rate or the cost of money

Y. Venugopal Reddy claims that price stability and growth have always been the main objectives of Indian monetary policy. The RBI has been granted the exclusive right to issue currency in order to maintain control over the money supply and credit. Control over the supply of currency and deposit money is referred to as control over the money supply. Therefore, one of the RBI's most significant functions is to regulate the amount of money. Based on reserves held in the form of foreign securities, gold bullion, rupee securities, and treasury bills, the RBI is authorized to create currency notes. It must always keep reserves of foreign exchange and gold totaling Rs 200 crore, of which Rs 115 crore must be in gold reserves.

**Price stability or inflation control-**

Rangarajan quotes that choosing the right target or objective for each investment is a constant challenge. Perhaps the most feasible goal for monetary authorities to achieve among the others is price stability. The primary goal of monetary policy is price stability. This is about keeping inflation at a manageable level that supports economic expansion. In a nation like India, structural changes brought about by economic expansion may lead to shifts in relative prices; as a result, inflationary pressures are unavoidable. In order to support the growth process, the RBI's duty in this situation would be to maintain a sustainable rate of inflation through its monetary policy.

The Central Bank may choose to take direct action in one of two ways: either by refusing to re-discount for banks whose credit policies are thought to be at odds with maintaining stable credit conditions. Even in that case, the Commercial Banks defy the Central Bank's constitutionally granted authority to order their closure. Only when the Central Bank is sufficiently strong and maintains friendly ties with the Commercial Banks will this approach prove effective. Generally speaking, the Central Bank is not frequently obliged to oppose such actions.

### Economic Growth

It is yet another crucial goal of monetary policy. It can encourage economic expansion by guaranteeing sufficient loan availability at reduced rates. To guarantee steady economic growth, both the short-term money market and long-term credit should be strengthened. The RBI increased CRR and SLR levels in accordance with the tight money policy. Later on, the repo and bank rates were higher, which impeded economic expansion. The earlier tight money policy was in opposition to the growth-promoting strategy. There has always been a case made for keeping inflation at 4% annually while expanding the money supply and improving market accessibility to credit in order to ensure economic growth.

### Exchange rate stability

Up until 1991, India maintained a fixed exchange rate regime and occasionally devalued its own currency with IMF agreement. Following liberalization, India established a floating currency rate, which resulted in unstable rupee exchange rates. The foreign exchange of the rupee has fluctuated due to variations in supply and demand for foreign exchange as well as changes in capital inflows and outflows.

In order to address such circumstances, the RBI could raise bank and repo rates, which would raise lending rates. Additionally, it increases CRR in order to lessen bank liquidity, which in turn lowers demand for foreign currency and balances the volatility of the foreign exchange market.

**Objectives of monetary policy-**

1. **Control Inflation:** Maintaining price stability by preventing excessive inflation or deflation.

2. **Manage Employment Levels:** Achieving low unemployment rates.

3. **Stabilize the Currency:** Ensuring a stable exchange rate.

4. **Promote Economic Growth:** Encouraging sustainable economic growth.

5. **Balance of Payments:** Ensuring a favorable balance of payments situation.

**Types of Monetary Policy**

**1 Expansionary Monetary Policy:**

**Objective:** Stimulate economic growth by increasing the money supply and lowering interest rates.

**Tools:** Lowering the policy interest rate, purchasing government securities, reducing reserve requirements.

**Effects:** Increased consumer spending and investment, higher demand for goods and services, potential risk of inflation.

### 2 Contractionary Monetary Policy:

**Objective:** Curb inflation by decreasing the money supply and raising interest rates.

**Tools:** Raising the policy interest rate, selling government securities, increasing reserve requirements.

**Effects:** Reduced consumer spending and investment, lower demand for goods and services, risk of increased unemployment.

### Tools of Monetary Policy

### 1 Open Market Operations (OMOs):

**Description:** Buying and selling government securities in the open market to regulate the money supply.

**Expansionary:** Central bank buys securities, increasing the money supply.

**Contractionary:** Central bank sells securities, decreasing the money supply.

### 2 Policy Interest Rates:

**Description:** Central bank sets the benchmark interest rates (e.g., repo rate, discount rate) to influence other interest rates in the economy.

**Expansionary:** Lowering interest rates to make borrowing cheaper.

**Contractionary:** Raising interest rates to make borrowing more expensive.

### 3  Reserve Requirements:

**Description:** The minimum amount of reserves that banks must hold against deposits.

**Expansionary:** Lowering reserve requirements to increase the funds available for lending.

**Contractionary:** Raising reserve requirements to decrease the funds available for lending.

### 4  Discount Rate:

**Description:** The interest rate charged by the central bank on loans to commercial banks.

**Expansionary:** Lowering the discount rate to encourage banks to borrow more and lend more.

**Contractionary:** Raising the discount rate to discourage borrowing by banks.

### 5  Moral Suasion:

**Description:** Central bank's use of persuasive techniques to influence and guide banking institutions to achieve desired economic outcomes.

**Methods:** Meetings, speeches, and directives.

### Case Study 3

### Apple Incorporation

Apple Inc., one of the world's leading technology companies, is highly sensitive to changes in monetary policy due to its large cash reserves, international operations, and significant investments in research and development.

Low Interest Rates (Post-2008 Financial Crisis):

Apple took advantage of low interest rates by issuing bonds, even though it had substantial cash reserves. The cheap borrowing costs allowed Apple to finance share buybacks and dividend payments without repatriating overseas cash, which would have incurred high taxes.

Example: In 2013, Apple issued $17 billion in bonds, the largest non-bank bond deal at the time, to fund shareholder returns.

Strategic Adaptations:

Diversifying its cash investments to optimize returns in varying interest rate environments.

Enhancing product innovation and expanding services to reduce dependency on hardware sales, thereby ensuring stable revenue streams irrespective of monetary policy shifts.

**Selective Credit Regulation**

Financing for particular uses or industries is regulated through selective and qualitative credit management. Selective credit controls deal with the distribution or flow of available credit supplies, whereas general credit controls deal with the cost and overall amount of credit. It should be noted that by granting exceptions to high-priority industries or endeavours, general credit regulations might likewise acquire a degree of selectivity. In India, this has been done frequently.

Selective controls are intended to deter activities that are deemed less desirable or comparatively unnecessary. In the Western countries, selective credit limitations have been implemented to keep inflationary pressure at bay in the event that demand for durable consumer goods exceeds supply. They have also been used to control credit in the stock market in the United States. Such restrictions have been implemented in India to stop speculative stockpiling of goods like food grains and necessary raw materials in an effort to stop an unwarranted increase in their costs. Several central banks now have the authority to directly regulate the entire amount of credit as well as the distribution of advances and investments made by individual banks and the banking system as a whole, in addition to the ability to impose selective credit controls.

It is believed that selective credit restrictions are a beneficial addition to overall credit regulation.

Based on the existing data, it seems that when combined with general credit regulations, their efficacy is significantly increased. They are made especially to prevent excesses in a certain area without having an impact on other credit kinds. By controlling the amount of bank credit available for the purchase and holding of specific commodities, they aim to bring about a satisfactory stabilization of their prices on the demand side. However, it should be remembered that supply and demand interact to set prices, and thus selective credit limitations are more likely to attenuate price increases rather than halt fundamental trends when supply is significantly limited.

Additionally, the Reserve Bank has the authority to occasionally issue directives to banking companies as a whole or to any specific banking company, depending on what it believes is best for the public interest, banking policy, preventing any banking company's operations from being run in a way that is harmful to the interests of its depositors, safeguarding the proper management of any banking company generally, or any combination of these. These instructions must be followed by the banking firms or the banking company, as the case may be.

In addition, the Reserve Bank has the authority to advise any banking firm generally and to warn or forbid any banking company specifically from engaging in any certain transaction or class of operations.

The Reserve Bank has occasionally requested in its circular letters that banks use caution when making loans in general and when lending against certain shares and commodities as collateral. Typically employed: (a) Minimum margins for lending against particular securities; (b) Credit ceilings for specified objectives; and (c) Differential interest rates on particular loans.

In India, the three methods are used to implement selective credit limitations. Generally, effort is taken to ensure that credit for production, the flow of commodities, and exports are not impacted when selection controls are imposed. The primary focus of selective controls is on credit to merchants who finance inventory.

## Case Study 4

Toyota Motor Corporation

Background: Toyota, a global automotive leader, is significantly affected by monetary policy due to its capital-intensive nature and reliance on consumer financing for vehicle purchases.

Low Interest Rates and QE:

In Japan, the Bank of Japan's (BOJ) prolonged low interest rates and QE measures aimed at combating deflation directly benefited Toyota. Lower borrowing costs made financing cheaper for both the company and its customers.

Toyota could finance its operations and expansion at a lower cost, while consumers found vehicle loans more affordable, boosting sales.

Strategic Adaptations:

Toyota increased its focus on localizing production in key markets to mitigate the impact of exchange rate volatility.

Enhanced its financial services division to provide attractive financing options, capitalizing on low interest rates to stimulate sales.

## Case Study 5

JPMorgan Chase & Co.

Background: JPMorgan Chase, one of the largest global financial institutions, is directly influenced by monetary policy through its impact on interest rates, liquidity, and overall economic conditions.

Strategic Adaptations:

Diversified revenue streams by expanding investment banking, asset management, and wealth management services to reduce reliance on traditional lending.

Implemented robust risk management practices to navigate rate changes and maintain financial stability.

## Fiscal Policy

Fiscal policy refers to the use of government spending and taxation to influence the economy. It is a crucial tool for managing economic performance, particularly in terms of promoting sustainable growth, reducing unemployment, and controlling inflation. The area of government policy known as fiscal policy is focused on determining the amount and direction of spending as well as generating revenue through taxes and other sources.

Via the budget, fiscal policy is implemented. The budget, which is often presented to parliament by the finance minister (in the case of a union budget) is an estimate of government spending and revenue for the next fiscal year.

The revenue (receipts) and expenditure (disbursements) sections of the budget are separated vertically. It is split into income account and capital account horizontally. As a result, the receipts are divided into Capital and Revenue Receipts, while the disbursements are divided into Capital and Revenue Expenditures.

All current administrative expenses of the government are included in the revenue expenditure, and all capital transactions of the government are included in the capital expenditure.

Tax money is included in the revenue receipts category, whereas market loans, foreign aid, repayment income, and other revenues—such as income from public undertakings—fall under the capital receipts category.

State governments have their own budgets, much like the federal government does.

The sources of revenue for the Union and the States are designated under the Indian Constitution.

According to the Indian Constitution, a Finance Commission must also be established every five years, or sooner if the President deems it necessary, in order to recommend to the President on matters pertaining to sound financial management, including the principles that should guide the distribution of grants-in-aid to states that require assistance from the Consolidated Fund of India, the allocation of net proceeds from taxes between the Union and States, and any other matters referred to the Commission by the President.

**Components of Fiscal Policy:**

**1 Government Spending (Expenditure):**

**Types:**

**Capital Expenditure:** Investments in infrastructure, education, and other long-term assets.

**Current Expenditure:** Day-to-day operational costs such as salaries, subsidies, and welfare payments.

**Impact:** Directly influences aggregate demand. Increased government spending can stimulate economic activity, while decreased spending can slow it down.

## 2 Taxation:

**Types:**

**Direct Taxes:** Taxes on income, profits, and wealth (e.g., income tax, corporate tax).

**Indirect Taxes:** Taxes on goods and services (e.g., sales tax, VAT).

**Impact:** Affects disposable income of individuals and businesses, thus influencing consumption and investment. Lower taxes can increase spending and investment, while higher taxes can reduce it.

**Objectives of Fiscal Policy:**

1 **Economic Growth:** Stimulate economic activity through strategic spending and tax incentives.

2 **Employment:** Reduce unemployment by creating jobs through public works and incentives for private sector employment.

3 **Price Stability:** Control inflation by managing demand through spending and tax policies.

4 **Economic Stability:** Stabilize the economy by mitigating the effects of economic cycles (recessions and booms).

**5 Redistribution of Income:** Use progressive taxation and welfare programs to reduce economic inequalities.

### Types of Fiscal Policy:

**1 Expansionary Fiscal Policy:**

**Objective:** Boost economic growth.

**Methods:** Increase government spending, decrease taxes, or both.

**Use:** Typically employed during recessions to stimulate demand.

**2 Contractionary Fiscal Policy:**

**Objective:** Slow down economic growth.

**Methods:** Decrease government spending, increase taxes, or both.

**Use:** Typically employed during periods of high inflation to reduce demand.

### Fiscal Policy Tools:

1 **Public Spending Programs:** Investments in infrastructure, education, healthcare, and other public goods.
2 **Tax Policies:** Adjustments in tax rates, tax credits, and deductions.
3 **Subsidies:** Financial assistance to support certain industries or economic activities.

4. **4Transfer Payments:** Welfare programs, unemployment benefits, pensions, and other forms of direct aid.

## Challenges in Implementing Fiscal Policy:

1. **Timing:** Delays in the implementation of fiscal measures can reduce their effectiveness.

2. **Political Constraints:** Political considerations can affect decision-making and the scope of fiscal measures.

3. **Budget Deficits and Public Debt:** Excessive government spending without adequate revenue can lead to large deficits and growing public debt.

4. **Crowding Out Effect:** Large government borrowing can lead to higher interest rates, potentially reducing private investment.

5. **Supply-Side Limitations:** While fiscal policy can influence demand, it might be less effective in addressing supply-side constraints such as productivity and labor market issues.

## Fiscal Policy in Practice:

**Keynesian Perspective:** Advocates for active fiscal policy to manage demand and address economic downturns.

**Classical Perspective:** Emphasizes limited government intervention, arguing that markets are self-correcting.

**Modern Considerations:** Focus on fiscal sustainability, structural reforms, and coordination with monetary policy.

**Recent Trends:**

**Response to Economic Crises:** Increased use of fiscal stimulus packages during economic downturns (e.g., 2008 financial crisis, COVID-19 pandemic).

**Sustainable Development Goals (SDGs):** Aligning fiscal policy with goals for sustainable and inclusive growth.

**Fiscal Rules:** Implementation of rules to ensure fiscal discipline, such as balanced budget requirements and debt ceilings.

**Conclusion:** Fiscal policy remains a vital tool for economic management, offering mechanisms to address various macroeconomic challenges. However, its effectiveness depends on timely implementation, political will, and careful consideration of long-term fiscal sustainability.

### Employment

Employment in India is a crucial aspect of the country's economic and social development. With a large and diverse population, the Indian labor market encompasses various sectors, types of employment, and challenges.

## Key Characteristics of Employment in India

### 1 Labor Force:

**Size and Growth:** India has one of the largest labor forces in the world, with significant growth driven by its young population.

**Labor Force Participation Rate:** Varies widely by gender, with male participation significantly higher than female participation.

### 2 Sectoral Distribution:

**Agriculture:** Traditionally the largest employer, although its share has been decreasing with structural changes in the economy.

**Industry:** Includes manufacturing, construction, and mining; experiencing moderate growth.

**Services:** Rapidly growing sector, contributing the most to GDP and employment in urban areas.

### 3 Types of Employment:

**Formal Employment:** Jobs with legal contracts, regular wages, and social security benefits; relatively small proportion of the total employment.

**Informal Employment:** Majority of the workforce; includes unregistered and unregulated jobs without formal contracts or benefits.

## Employment Trends

### 1  Rural vs. Urban Employment:

**Rural Employment:** Dominated by agriculture and allied activities; issues of underemployment and low productivity.

**Urban Employment:** Growing in the services and industrial sectors; includes higher levels of formal employment.

### 2  Unemployment Rates:

**Overall Unemployment:** Varies with economic cycles; influenced by factors like economic policies, global market conditions, and technological changes.

**Youth Unemployment:** Higher rates compared to the general population; challenges include skill mismatch and lack of job opportunities.

### 3  Underemployment:

Significant issue, especially in rural areas, where individuals may work less than full time or in jobs that do not utilize their skills fully.

Government Initiatives and Programs

### 1  Employment Generation Programs:

**Mahatma Gandhi National Rural Employment Guarantee Act (MGNREGA):** Provides 100 days of guaranteed wage employment to rural households.

**Pradhan Mantri Rojgar Protsahan Yojana (PMRPY):** Incentivizes employers to generate new employment by contributing to social security schemes for new employees.

## 2 Skill Development Initiatives:

Skill India Mission: Aims to train over 400 million people in various skills by 2022.

Pradhan Mantri Kaushal Vikas Yojana (PMKVY): Offers short-term training and skill certification.

## 3 Startup and Entrepreneurship Support:

**Startup India:** Encourages innovation and entrepreneurship by providing financial support, ease of doing business, and networking opportunities.

## 4 Urban Employment Schemes:

**Deen Dayal Antyodaya Yojana-National Urban Livelihoods Mission (DAY-NULM):** Enhances employment opportunities for urban poor through skill development and entrepreneurship support.

## Challenges

## 1 Informal Sector Dominance:

A large proportion of the workforce is employed in informal jobs, lacking job security, benefits, and social protection.

## 2 Skill Mismatch:

Discrepancy between the skills possessed by the workforce and those demanded by the market; contributes to high unemployment among educated youth.

## 3  Gender Disparities:

Significant gender gaps in labor force participation, wages, and working conditions; societal norms and lack of supportive infrastructure are major barriers.

## 4  Rural-Urban Divide:

Disparities in employment opportunities, income levels, and access to resources between rural and urban areas.

## 5  Technological Disruption:

Automation and digitalization pose a threat to traditional jobs, necessitating reskilling and adaptation to new job roles.

# Industrial Policy 1991

The Industrial Policy of 1948 was the first document outlining India's industrialization strategy. The Industries (Development and Regulation Act) was created by the state in 1951 as a step towards India's industrialization. India's industrialization began with the execution of the second five-year plan, which prompted the government to create the new Industrial Policy in 1956.

The Act's primary goals were to provide the government more authority:

(i) To take the required actions to promote the growth of industries;

(ii) To control the course and pattern of industrial growth;

(iii) To regulate industrial endeavours in the public interest in terms of their performance, activities, and outcomes.

Prior to 1991's liberalisation, the private sector's influence in India, especially that of major firms, was mostly restricted. 17 of the most significant industries were set aside for state development. The state was to play a role in the creation of another twelve important industries. Cooperatives, joint-stock companies, and small businesses were to be given preference over large private sector entrepreneurs in the remaining industries.

Furthermore, the small-scale industry was the only one allowed to produce a considerable quantity of things. Entry and expansion were controlled by licencing and, in the case of some major company categories, the MRTP Act, even for businesses that were open to the private sector. As a result, the government policy restricted the potential for private enterprise. But the July 1991 policy change drastically altered the business environment by opening up all but a few industries to the private sector. Prior to the liberalization of trade, government policies severely limited the growth and portfolio plans of businesses.

On July 24, 1991, the new administration led by Shri Narasimha Rao unveiled a series of liberalisation initiatives as part of its Industrial Policy. "Build on the gains already made, correct the distortions or weaknesses that may have crept in, maintain a sustained growth in productivity and gainful employment and attain international competitiveness" was the stated goal of the policy, which aimed to boost the industrial sector. The pursuit of these goals will lessen the need to protect the environment and make sure that resources are used effectively.

The broad objectives of New Industrial Policy 1991 are as follows:

(i) Freeing the sector from restrictions like licences and regulations.

(ii) Strengthening assistance for the small-scale industry

(iii) Increasing industry competitiveness to the general public's advantage.

(iv) Ensuring public companies operate like businesses in order to reduce losses.

(v) Offering greater incentives for the industrialization of the underdeveloped regions, and

(vi) Ensuring quick industrial growth in a cutthroat market.

Government Initiatives

Industrial licensing policy

(i) The Industries (Development & Regulation) Act, 1951 governs industrial licencing. A number of adjustments to the industrial approvals system were required in order to meet the goals of the industrial sector policy. With the exception of the 18 industries listed in Annexure II of the ID & R Act (1951), the Industrial Licence Requirement has been eliminated by the IPR 1991, regardless of the amount of investment in any industry. Industries such as coal, lignite, petroleum, sugar, cigarettes, automobiles, hazardous chemicals, medicines, asbestos, plywood and other wood-based products, newsprint, electronics, and some luxury goods are among those where industrial licencing will be required. Only five industries—alcohol, cigarettes, dangerous chemicals, electronics, aircraft and defence equipment, and industrial explosions—need licences.

(ii) Foreign Investment It has been determined to approve direct foreign investment up to 51% foreign equity in high priority industries that demand significant capital and cutting edge technology in order to facilitate foreign investment in these sectors. This method will not encounter any form of bottlenecks. FERA businesses are already permitted to make discretionary investments in this set of industries, which is commonly referred to as the "Appendix I Industries." Therefore, the main modifications to the foreign investment regime were the following: a case-by-case evaluation of applications for foreign equity ownership up to 75% in nine sectors, mostly related to infrastructure, and automatic approval of FDI up to 51% of equity ownership by foreign firms in a group of 34 technology-intensive industries.

(iii) Foreign Technology Agreements Given the importance of technological dynamism in Indian industry today, the government would automatically approve technology agreements relating to high priority industries as long as they fall within predetermined bounds. Increased competitive pressure will also drive industry to invest significantly more in R&D. To support this effort, prior clearance will no longer be required for individual foreign technician hires or foreign technology testing of domestically developed technologies, either as part of an industrial or investment approval process or otherwise. Under assigned authorities administered by the RBI, or by the government, foreign technology cooperation are allowed through the automatic method. Cases pertaining to industrial licences and small-scale reserved items, on the other hand, are not eligible for automatic clearance and must be reviewed and approved by the government.

Automatic approval: The Reserve Bank of India grants automatic approval to all industries for foreign technology collaboration agreements through its regional offices, provided that the following conditions are met: lump sum payments cannot exceed US $2 million; royalty payable cannot exceed 5% for domestic sales and 8% for exports, with a total payment of 8% on sales over a ten-year period; and the royalty payment period cannot exceed seven years from the date of commercial production commencement or ten years from the agreement's date, whichever is earlier. The royalty limits mentioned above are net of taxes and are computed using standard conditions.

**(iv)** Public sector policy In eight key areas, the public sector will continue to hold a dominant position. These include firearms and ammo, nuclear energy, mineral oils, railway transportation, and coal and mineral mining. Mining was taken off the licencing

Foreign Technology Agreements:

**Liberalization**

India's economic liberalization refers to the current reforms taking place in the country. Following its 1947 independence, India adopted socialist programs. The heavy regulation was mockingly referred to as the "Licence Raj" and the sluggish rate of growth as the "Hindu rate of growth". Prime Minister Rajiv Gandhi started a few changes in the 1980s. Politics stood in the way of his administration. Following the International Monetary Fund's (IMF) 1991 bailout of the bankrupt state, P. V. Narasimha Rao's government, led by his Finance Minister Manmohan Singh, initiated ground-breaking reforms. The new policies included deregulation, the start of privatization, opening up trade and investment with other countries, tax reforms, and steps to control inflation. Since then, the general course of liberalization has not changed, regardless of the party in power; nevertheless, no party has attempted to confront influential groups like farmers' associations and trade unions, or controversial topics like changing labor regulations and cutting back on agricultural subsidies.

**Commercialization**

The process of bringing a state-owned or public sector enterprise under private ownership or management is known as privatization. More broadly, it means introducing private administration and control into PSUs, even in the absence of a shift in ownership. According to

Barbara Lee and John Nellis (1990), privatisation is the process of bringing the private sector into the ownership and management of a state-owned business. Hence, the phrase describes the private acquisition of all or a portion of a business. It includes management contracting out and privatisation through leases, franchise agreements, or management contracts.

Privatisation can manifest itself in the following ways:

Measures of Ownership: The amount of ownership that is moved from the public sector to the private sector determines the level of privatization. It may appear as one of the following:

Complete Denationalization: This refers to the full handover of a public company to the private sector.

As demonstrated in BALCO, which Sterlite Industries purchased. Hindustan Lever purchased Modern Foods.

Joint Venture: This suggests introducing private ownership to some extent. Private ownership might range from as little as 25% to as much as 75% or higher. Similar to Maruti Suzuki, where Maruti had previously held the majority of the shares, Suzuki boosted its position following deregulation to take the lead in terms of ownership.

Worldwide Integration

Creating in a Global Setting

If overseeing product development procedures was difficult in the past, it is becoming more difficult now that businesses are pursuing global design approaches. The cost advantages of global designing are highly alluring to modern manufacturers; nevertheless, they also bring with them additional obstacles related to Product Lifecycle Management (PLM) and exacerbate pre-existing issues such as intellectual property protection.

## Questions

| Question | Option 1 | Option 2 | Option 3 | Option 4 | Answer |
|---|---|---|---|---|---|
| Name the low income economies | First world | Second world | Third world | None of these | 3 |
| Select the Govt.'s strategy in respect of public expenditure and revenue which have a significant impact on business. | Monetary policy | Fiscal Policy | Trade policy | Foreign exchange policy | 2 |
| Identify the policy that is concerned with raising | Monetary policy | Fiscal Policy | Trade policy | Foreign exchange policy | 2 |

| | | | | | |
|---|---|---|---|---|---|
| revenue through taxation and deciding on the level and pattern of expenditure | | | | | |
| Identify the person who is responsible for presenting the Union Budget before the Parliament | Prime Minister | Finance Minister | RBI Governor | None of these | 2 |
| Predict the benefit of exploring to foreign markets | It protects them against foreign competition | It cushions them from the effects of events in other countries | It opens up new market opportunities | It increases the risk and uncertainty of operating in globalizing world economy | 3 |

| Indicate the nature of an environment that is increasingly complex and turbulent displays | More orderly competition | More predictable demand | A reduced risk of product obsolescence | Increased speed of innovation | 4 |
|---|---|---|---|---|---|
| Select the Industrial Policy Resolution (IPR) that is known as Economic Constitution of India. | IPR 1964 | IPR 1976 | IPR 1956 | IPR 1948 | 3 |
| Select the IP that abolished the Industrial licensing | IPR 1956 | IPR 1964 | IPR 1991 | IPR 1977 | 3 |
| Indicate the full form of EPZ | Export Processing Zone | Export Promotion Zone | External Promotion zone | None of these | 1 |

| | | | | | |
|---|---|---|---|---|---|
| Select the activity that is concerned with the obligation and duties of business to the society | Social responsibility | Status | Authority | None of these | 1 |
| Select the type of securities those are bought and sold in open market operation | Pvt. Securities | Govt. securities | Initial securities | None of these | 2 |
| Indicate the Bill that is concerned with the tax proposals of the Budget | Cash Bill | Finance Bill | State Bill | None of these | 2 |
| Predict the item of the budget that is | Capital expenditure | Revenue expenditure | Deferred expenditure | None of these | 2 |

| | | | | | |
|---|---|---|---|---|---|
| concerned with the current expenditure of Govt. on administration | | | | | |
| Indicate the full form of CSR | Company Social Responsibility | Corporate Social Rights | Corporate Social Responsibility | Company Social Rights | 3 |
| Predict the benefit that is derived from competitive rivalry | Price war | Differentiation | Alliances | Higher marketing budgets | 2 |
| Select the proper acronym of PESTLE | Political, environmental, technological, legal, and environmental | Political, environmental, shareholding, technological, logistical, and e-marketing | Political, economic, social, technological, legal, and environmental | Political, environmental, societal, technological, learning, and e-marketing | 3 |
| Indicate the nature of activity enumerat | External regulation | Self-regulation | Government control | Charitable action | 2 |

| ed in corporate governance | | | | | |
|---|---|---|---|---|---|
| | | | | | |

| |
|---|
| Describe the term 'Public Investment'. |
| Describe public expenditure. |
| Describe fiscal policy. |
| Describe monetary policy. |
| Describe components of money demand. |
| Describe Government role in money demand. |
| Describe investors' role in money demand. |
| Describe role of general public in money demand. |
| Describe money supply. |
| Describe role of RBI in money supply. |

# Chapter 3
# Banking Infrastructure For Economic Development

**CHAPTER CONTENT**

Reserve Bank of India
RBI and Monetary Policy
Commercial Banking

## Reserve Bank Of India

In compliance with the regulations outlined in the Reserve Bank of India Act, 1934, the Reserve Bank of India was founded on April 1, 1935. The Reserve Bank's Central Office was first located in Calcutta before being permanently relocated to Mumbai in 1937. The Governor's office and the policy-making department are located in the Central Office. Initially, non-government shareholders held nearly all of the company's share capital. Therefore, on January 1, 1949, the RBI was nationalized in order to stop the concentration of shares in a small number of hands. The nation's central bank is called the Reserve Bank of India (RBI). A statutory body is the RBI. It is in charge of controlling the supply and producing currency notes.

RBI functions are as follows—

1. The Reserve Bank of India: Has the only authority to print money notes, with the exception of rupee notes, which are printed by the Ministry of Finance. All around the nation, Reserve Bank of India currency notes are regarded as limitless legal tender. The Indian government issues coins, one-rupee notes, and tiny coins. The "managed paper currency standard" has been embraced by India.

2. Banker to the government: With the exception of Jammu and Kashmir, the RBI serves as a banker to both the national government of India and the state governments. It is responsible for managing and keeping up the government's bank accounts. It gathers money receipts and disburses payments on the government's behalf. As an IMF and World Bank member, it speaks for the Indian government.

The RBI serves as the government of India's lender and extends short-term loans. Treasury bills can be sold to obtain this short-term credit. Additionally, RBI offers State Governments ways and means of advances (repayable in 90 days). It should be mentioned that the RBI grants the Central Government the authority to borrow any amount it desires.

3. Banker's bank: The RBI lends money to commercial banks on a short-term basis while holding a portion of their cash reserves. A fixed percentage of total liabilities must be maintained by all banks. The RBI's primary goal in adjusting this cash reserve ratio is to manage credit. Through the rediscounting of bills of exchange, the RBI

offers financial support to State cooperative banks and commercial banks. The RBI is mandated by law to oversee, manage, and exert control over the operations of commercial and cooperative banks. The RBI requests returns and relevant data from banks during routine inspections.

4. Exchange management and control: As mandated by RBI Act section 40, it is responsible for upholding the rupee's external value. The country's innate economic strength, the manner in which it manages its monetary and economic affairs, and the external stability of the currency are all strongly correlated. Maintaining the currency's foreign value is mostly dependent on domestic, fiscal, and monetary policy. The Reserve Bank of India is a key player in this field. The RBI is able to transact foreign exchange on behalf of the government as well as for its own account.

5. Credit control: To further the interests of the nation, the RBI regulates the total amount of money in circulation and bank credits. To maintain price and exchange rate stability, the RBI regulates credit. The RBI uses all available credit control tools, including selective, qualitative, and quantitative controls, to accomplish this. The bank rate is the credit tool that the RBI uses the most frequently. The selective methods of credit control are also heavily relied upon by the RBI.

6. Lender of Last Resort – When commercial banks need help getting through a financial crisis, they turn to the Reserve Bank, which helps them out even though it may demand a higher interest rate.

7. Bank Rate This credit control approach is the oldest. Up to the start of World War I, the Bank of England was the one to launch it. The rate at which the central bank rediscounts first-class bills of exchange and government securities held by commercial banks is known as the bank rate, sometimes known as the discount rate. The interest rate that the central bank charges banks at which it offers them a rediscount through the discount window is known as the bank rate. By changing the bank rate, the central bank manages credit.

The central bank reduces the bank rate in order to increase credit. The central bank becomes a cheap and convenient source of borrowing. The commercial banks will thereby take on greater debt. They will then provide loans to clients at lower interest rate.

8. Open Market Operation: The most recent time saw the emergence of OMO as a credit control tool when the central bank perceived bank rate policy as a flimsy tool. In order to increase or decrease the amount of money in the banking system, it refers to the purchasing and selling of government securities on the open market.

OMO refers to a nation's central bank buying and selling securities. The Central Bank's sale of securities causes credit to decline, while its acquisition causes credit to expand.

The nation's central bank uses an open market operation as one tool to control the amount of money in circulation. The central bank can buy or sell government bonds on the open market by using OMOs.

9 Cash Reserve Ratio It is the most straightforward and efficient way to manage credit. Commercial banks' surplus reserves have two possible outcomes: they can be completely eliminated or rendered useless for creating credit. It is referred to as Variable CRR and is caused by changes in a commercial bank's cash reserve ratio.

Lord Keynes was the one who first proposed this approach. This approach is regarded as a vital resource for enhancing the financial system's overall liquidity and solvency. In addition to fostering public trust in commercial banks' ability to fulfil deposit obligations, this system was first used in the United States in 1933 as a means of regulating the amount of credit available to the banking sector.

Every commercial bank was required by the RBI Act of 1934 to maintain a minimum amount of cash reserves with the RBI. At first, it was set at 5% for demand deposits and 2% for time deposits. The RBI was given the authority to change the amount of cash reserves required in 1962, from 3% to 15% of total demand and time deposits.

The Narasimhan Committee opposed the use of CRR as a tool to reduce inflation. From 15% in 1994–1995 to 8% in 2000–01, the CRR was progressively decreased until it reached 4%. In 2008, it increased once more to 8% in an effort to fight inflation; over time, it has stabilised around 4%. CRR is now only 3%.

10 SLR- A minimum statutory liquidity ratio (SLR) of 25% of the banks' net demand and time obligations is required by the Banking Regulation Act of 1962. It allows

the RBI to raise this ratio to 40% in order to regulate liquidity if needed. The authority to establish SLR for commercial banks is granted to the RBI.

In 1991, SLR accounted for 38.5% of a commercial bank's net demand and time liabilities. In response to the recommendations of the Narsimhan Committee, the government agreed in 2012 to further lower the SLR from 38.5% to 25%.

11 Control of InflationThe Reserve Bank of India (RBI) is the central bank of the country and plays a crucial role in maintaining economic stability. One of its primary responsibilities is to control inflation, which involves managing the rate at which the general level of prices for goods and services rises.

## RBI And Monetary Policy

Since its founding, the RBI has adhered to the policy of managed expansion, which calls for sufficient funding of economic expansion while maintaining appropriate price stability. In developing nations, increased financial resources are necessary for investment and development. But inflation is the outcome of this expansion. Thus, in order to strike a balance between expansion and inflation, the RBI must exercise caution. In addition, as market forces now determine the currency rate following liberalization, the RBI also controls the foreign exchange rate through open market operations.

One could argue that the main focus of monetary policy is the gradual increase in bank credit and the money supply, paying particular attention to the seasonal fluctuations in credit needs. The quantity of bank credits and the money supply are viewed by the RBI as the two main intermediate variables, and it uses the latter to try and influence the former. It is believed that changes in bank credit are the fundamental cause of the money supply's fluctuations rather than the money supply changing on its own.

**Credit Control and the RBI**

The RBI uses direct intervention, reserve requirement modifications, open market operations, bank rate manipulation, loan rationing, and moral persuasion to restrict credit. In addition to using these conventional techniques for credit control, it has a direct impact on the lending policies, interest rates, types of securities used as collateral against loans, and portfolio allocation of commercial banks.

**1 Monetary Policy:**

The primary tool through which the RBI controls inflation is monetary policy. The central bank uses various instruments to regulate the money supply and influence interest rates in the economy.

**2 Repo Rate:**

**Definition:** The rate at which the RBI lends money to commercial banks.

**Inflation Control:** By increasing the repo rate, the RBI makes borrowing more expensive, reducing the money supply and curbing consumer spending and investment, which helps to reduce inflationary pressures.

## 3 Reverse Repo Rate:

**Definition:** The rate at which the RBI borrows money from commercial banks.

**Inflation Control:** By increasing the reverse repo rate, the RBI encourages banks to park more funds with it, reducing the money available in the economy, which helps in controlling inflation.

## 4 Cash Reserve Ratio (CRR):

**Definition:** The percentage of a bank's total deposits that must be maintained with the RBI as reserves.

**Inflation Control:** Increasing the CRR reduces the amount of funds available for banks to lend, thereby decreasing the money supply and controlling inflation.

## 5 Statutory Liquidity Ratio (SLR):

**Definition:** The percentage of a bank's net demand and time liabilities that must be maintained in the form of liquid assets.

**Inflation Control:** Raising the SLR reduces the funds available for banks to extend as loans, which helps in controlling the money supply and inflation.

## 6 Open Market Operations (OMOs):

**Definition:** The buying and selling of government securities in the open market by the RBI.

**Inflation Control:** Selling government securities absorbs excess liquidity from the market, reducing the money supply and helping to control inflation.

# Commercial Banking

Commercial banks are financial institutions that provide a wide range of services including accepting deposits, providing loans, and offering various financial products to individuals, businesses, and governments. In India, commercial banks play a pivotal role in the economy by facilitating financial transactions, supporting economic growth, and ensuring financial stability.

## Types of Commercial Banks in India

### 1 Public Sector Banks:

**Definition:** Banks where the majority stake is held by the government.

**Examples:** State Bank of India (SBI), Punjab National Bank (PNB), Bank of Baroda.

**Characteristics:** Largest market share, extensive branch network, government support.

### 2 Private Sector Banks:

**Definition:** Banks where the majority stake is held by private entities or individuals.

**Examples:** HDFC Bank, ICICI Bank, Axis Bank.

**Characteristics:** Focus on efficiency, customer service, and technology-driven services.

### 3 Foreign Banks:

**Definition:** Banks that are headquartered outside India but operate through branches or subsidiaries in India.

**Examples:** Citibank, HSBC, Standard Chartered.

**Characteristics:** Global operations, niche services, sophisticated technology.

### 4 Regional Rural Banks (RRBs):

**Definition:** Banks established to provide banking services in rural areas, sponsored by public sector banks.

**Examples:** Prathama Bank, Baroda Uttar Pradesh Gramin Bank.

**Characteristics:** Focus on agricultural and rural development, local presence.

### 5 Cooperative Banks:

**Definition:** Banks owned and operated by cooperative societies, catering primarily to the needs of small borrowers in rural and urban areas.

**Examples:** Saraswat Bank, Punjab and Maharashtra Cooperative Bank.

**Characteristics:** Member-driven, local focus, lower costs.

Functions of Commercial Banks

### 1 Accepting Deposits:

**Types of Deposits:** Savings accounts, current accounts, fixed deposits, recurring deposits.

**Purpose:** Mobilize savings from individuals and entities.

### 2 Providing Loans and Advances:

**Types of Loans:** Personal loans, home loans, business loans, agricultural loans.

**Purpose:** Support personal consumption, business expansion, and economic development.

### 3  Credit Creation:

**Mechanism:** Lending more than the initial deposits received, thereby creating additional money supply in the economy.

### 4  Payment and Settlement Services:

**Services:** Issuing cheque, electronic fund transfers, demand drafts, internet banking.

**Purpose:** Facilitate smooth financial transactions.

### 5  Investment Services:

**Products:** Mutual funds, fixed income securities, insurance products.

**Purpose:** Provide investment avenues to customers.

### 6  Foreign Exchange Transactions:

**Services:** Currency exchange, remittances, export and import financing.

**Purpose:** Support international trade and investment.

### 7  Financial Advisory Services:

**Advisory:** Wealth management, retirement planning, tax planning.

**Purpose:** Help customers make informed financial decisions.

Role of Commercial Banks in the Indian Economy

## 1 Economic Growth:

**Function:** Providing credit to various sectors including agriculture, industry, and services.

**Impact:** Drives investment, production, and employment.

## 2 Financial Inclusion:

**Initiatives:** Opening branches in unbanked areas, promoting digital banking, offering basic banking services.

**Impact:** Extends banking services to underbanked and unbanked populations.

## 3 Support to Government Policies:

**Implementation:** Executing government schemes like Jan Dhan Yojana, PMMY, and other financial inclusion programs.

**Impact:** Helps in achieving socio-economic goals.

## 4 Stabilizing Financial Systems:

**Function:** Maintaining liquidity and stability in the financial markets through prudent banking practices.

**Impact:** Ensures the stability and reliability of the financial system.

## Regulatory Framework

## 1 Reserve Bank of India (RBI):

**Role:** Central bank and primary regulator of commercial banks.

**Functions:** Issuing guidelines, conducting inspections, ensuring compliance with regulations.

## 2 Banking Regulation Act, 1949:

**Purpose:** Provides a framework for the regulation and supervision of commercial banks.

**Provisions:** Licensing, management, operations, and audits of banks.

## Case Study 6

## HDFC Bank

Background: HDFC Bank is one of India's leading private sector banks, known for its strong retail banking franchise and wide range of financial services.

Regulatory Environment: The Reserve Bank of India (RBI) imposes various regulations on banking operations, including capital adequacy norms, asset quality standards, and customer protection guidelines.

## Regulatory Impact:

Capital Adequacy Requirements:

The RBI mandates banks to maintain a minimum Capital to Risk (Weighted) Assets Ratio (CRAR) to ensure financial stability. HDFC Bank has consistently maintained a CRAR above the required threshold, ensuring robust capital buffers.

Compliance with Basel III norms, which require higher capital reserves and better risk management practices, has been a priority for HDFC Bank.

## Non-Performing Assets (NPA) Management:

The RBI's stringent norms on asset classification and provisioning for NPAs ensure that banks do not understate their financial risks. HDFC Bank has maintained relatively low NPAs compared to peers, thanks to prudent lending practices and effective risk management.

## Digital Banking Regulations:

The RBI's guidelines on digital payments and cybersecurity have prompted HDFC Bank to invest significantly in technology and security infrastructure. This includes robust KYC processes and advanced fraud detection systems to safeguard customer transactions.

## Strategic Adaptations:

HDFC Bank has leveraged its strong capital position to expand its lending and investment portfolios, focusing on high-growth sectors while maintaining asset quality.

The bank has invested in digital banking initiatives, enhancing customer experience through innovative products like mobile banking apps and contactless payment solutions.

## Case Study 7

## State Bank of India (SBI)

Background: SBI is India's largest public sector bank, with a significant presence in both urban and rural areas. It plays a crucial role in implementing government policies and financial inclusion initiatives.

Regulatory Environment: As a public sector bank, SBI is subject to extensive regulatory oversight by the RBI, especially concerning financial inclusion, priority sector lending, and corporate governance.

## Regulatory Impact:

### Priority Sector Lending (PSL):

RBI mandates that banks must allocate a certain percentage of their total lending to priority sectors such as agriculture, micro, small, and medium enterprises (MSMEs), and affordable housing. SBI has consistently met its PSL targets, contributing to economic development and financial inclusion.

### Corporate Governance and Transparency:

The RBI's emphasis on corporate governance requires banks to maintain transparency and accountability in their operations. SBI has adopted stringent governance practices, including regular audits, risk assessments, and adherence to disclosure norms.

### Financial Inclusion:

RBI's push for financial inclusion has led SBI to expand its branch network in rural areas and launch initiatives like the Pradhan Mantri Jan Dhan Yojana (PMJDY), aimed at providing banking services to the unbanked population.

## Strategic Adaptations:

SBI has developed tailored financial products and services to meet the needs of priority sectors, leveraging technology to improve access and efficiency.

The bank has enhanced its corporate governance framework, ensuring compliance with regulatory standards and fostering stakeholder trust.

## Case Study 8

## ICICI Bank

Background: ICICI Bank is a major private sector bank in India, known for its diverse financial services and innovative banking solutions.

Regulatory Environment: ICICI Bank operates under the stringent regulatory framework set by the RBI, which includes guidelines on capital adequacy, risk management, and consumer protection.

Regulatory Impact:

Risk Management:

RBI's regulations on risk management require banks to adopt comprehensive frameworks to identify, assess, and mitigate risks. ICICI Bank has implemented advanced risk management systems, including stress testing and scenario analysis, to ensure financial stability.

## Customer Protection:

RBI mandates various consumer protection measures, including transparency in loan pricing, grievance redressal mechanisms, and fair lending practices. ICICI

Bank has established robust customer service protocols and transparent communication strategies.

## Technological Innovation:

Regulations on digital banking and cybersecurity have driven ICICI Bank to adopt cutting-edge technologies and security measures. Compliance with guidelines on data privacy and transaction security is a top priority.

## Strategic Adaptations:

ICICI Bank has focused on diversifying its risk portfolio and enhancing its risk assessment models to comply with regulatory requirements and safeguard its financial health.

The bank has invested heavily in digital transformation, offering a suite of online banking services, mobile applications, and digital payment solutions to meet customer expectations and regulatory standards.

## Questions

| Question | Option 1 | Option 2 | Option 3 | Option 4 | Answer |
|---|---|---|---|---|---|
| Name the rate at which the central bank discounts or rediscounts | Credit rate | Bank rate | Bill rate | Deposit rate | 2 |

| the eligible bills | | | | | |
|---|---|---|---|---|---|
| Predict the process of transfer of asset from public sector to the private sector | Privatisation | Deregulation | Nationalisation | Individualisation | 1 |
| Predict the Branch of Govt. that is responsible for implementing or carrying out law and policy | The legislature | The executive | The Judiciary | The bureaucracy | 2 |
| Judge the main objective of macroeconomic policy | A high and stable level of employment | A low and stable rate of inflation | A stable and satisfactory rate of economy | All of these | 4 |
| Predict the inherent meaning of CSR | The same as business ethics | A theory about ethics | The integration of social and environme | The title of a Govt. Committee | 3 |

| | | | ntal concern in the daily business of the firm | | |
|---|---|---|---|---|---|
| Write the meaning of PPP or P3 initiative | Public policy papers | Public Private Partnership | Private Procurement Production | Personal Production Proposal | 2 |
| Predict the person who developed the Theory of Comparative Advantage | Adam Smith | David Richardo | Joseph stiglitz | Amartya Sen | 2 |
| Identify the sector that got priority in the 1st five-year plan | Agriculture | Industrial | Infrastructure | Communication | 1 |
| Predict the nature of Indian Economy | Capitalist economy | Closed economy | Mixed Economy | None of these | 3 |
| Indicate the economy that is free from any | Closed Economy | Mixed Economy | Free market economy | None of these | 3 |

| government intervention | | | | | |
|---|---|---|---|---|---|
| Indicate the outlook of Indian plans | Economic Growth | Industrial expansion | Growth with social justice | None of these | 3 |
| Predict the rate at which RBI borrows money from commercial bank | Repo Rate | Market rate of Interest | Inflation rate. | Reverse Repo rate | 4 |
| Predict the nature of Indian Economy prior to the 1990 | Export Substitution | Import Promotion | Export Promotion | Import Substitution | 4 |

| |
|---|
| Explain role of RBI in controlling inflation. |
| Explain role of RBI in controlling money supply. |
| Explain the role of Government of India in controlling fiscal deficit. |

| |
|---|
| Discuss effects of increasing interest rate in an economy. |
| Discuss effects of increasing bank rate in an economy. |

# Chapter 4
# Privatization, Globalization And Foreign Trade Policy

**CHAPTER CONTENT**

Privatization

Privatization in India

Disinvestment

Globalization

Foreign Trade

Foreign Trade Policy in India

## Privatizazion

The transfer of ownership and/or management of an enterprise from the public to the private sectors is known as privatization, and it has become a global trend. It also refers to the state's partial or whole disengagement from a sector or industry. Opening up a sector of the economy that has been restricted to the public sector to the private sector is another aspect of privatization.

The unchecked growth of the public sector and the ensuing issues have historically necessitated privatization. It evolved into an essential component of economic revival even in the so-called communist nations.

Divestment, or the privatization of ownership through the sale of equity, is a significant kind of privatization. In nations with robust capital markets, this means offering stock for sale to the general public. The main way that privatization has occurred in industrialized nations is through the sale of state-owned businesses.

Denationalization or privatization are two common ways that privatization manifests itself. Denationalization of a sizable number of businesses occurred in nations including Bangladesh, Pakistan, and Chile.

Contracting is an additional method of privatization. Governments have the authority to assign planned and specified services to other groups for production and delivery.

In the utilities and urban transport sectors, franchising—which permits the provision of certain services in predetermined geographic areas—is quite prevalent. In the fields of public works, defence, and several specialty services, contracts are typical. Contracting is effective when vendors compete for contracts and there is no loss of economies of scale. However, contracting can lead to corruption, and long-term agreements often encourage the private supplier to behave in a monopolistic manner.

Leases and management contracts can be used to privatize management, which is another way that privatization might occur.

The government may also release itself from the obligation by an official or informal liquidation.

## Objects

Boost the size and vibrancy of the private sector, hence increasing ownership distribution among the general public; and • Enhance PSU performance to mitigate the financial burden on taxpayers.

- To promote and assist private sector investments from both local and international sources.
- To bring in money for the state
- To lessen the state's administrative burden
- Starting and maintaining the shift in the economy's structure from a command to a market economy.

## Methods

Divestiture, or the privatization of ownership through equity sales, is one of the key methods of privatization.

- Privatization or denationalization.
- Contracting: In this method, services are produced and delivered by other organisations under contract from the government.
- In the utilities and urban transport sectors, franchising—which permits the provision of certain services in specified geographic areas—is quite widespread.

- The government ceasing to provide some goods and services, leaving the private sector to handle them entirely or in part.

- Letting management contracts and leases be used to privatize management

- Liquidation, which may occur in an informal or formal setting. A formal liquidation entails closing an organization and selling its assets. A company that enters an informal liquidation maintains its legal standing even if some or all of its activities are halted.

**Advantages**

The following is a possible summary of privatization's advantages:

- • By relieving the state of the SOEs' losses and cutting back on bureaucracy, it lessens the state's financial burden.

- • The government can raise money through the privatisation of SOEs.

- Privatization enables the government to reduce the amount of administrative apparatus.

- It allows the government to focus more on the vital duties of the state 24

- Because privatization draws more resources from the private sector for development, it quickens the rate of economic growth.

- It might lead to improved enterprise management.

- Privatization might promote entrepreneurship as well.

Privatization has the potential to increase the number of shareholders among the general public and workers. This might increase public scrutiny of the businesses.

## Arguments against privatization

The following are some significant arguments against privatization:

- • The public sector was created with some lofty goals in mind, and privatization entails doing away with them all at once.
- To everyone's disadvantage, privatization will promote the concentration of economic power.
- It will be extremely harmful if privatization leads to the monopolistic power of private firms replacing that of public enterprises.
- Oftentimes, privatization leads to foreign companies purchasing domestic companies.
- The government forfeits future revenue streams when profitable businesses, even potentially profitable ones, are privatized.
- It is against national interests to privatize important and strategic sectors.
- Both the public and private sectors contain both well-run and poorly run businesses. It is the caliber and dedication of the management, not the industry, that counts.

- Developing nations' capital markets aren't developed enough to handle privatisation effectively.

- Privatization is frequently an attempt at reform, and as such, it is not executed well. Because of this, it's possible that the desired outcomes won't be realized.

- Privatisation frequently has entrenched interests at play, which amounts to misleading the public. Privatization has frequently been a "garage sale" to favoured people and groups in many different countries.

**Requirement for success**

- Privatization cannot continue unless the political establishment is in favour of it and unless it signifies a change in public preferences brought about by discontent with the efficacy of other options.

- The public good may not be increased by substituting a private monopoly for a government monopoly; instead, there should be a variety of private suppliers.

- The private sector's provision of public services ought to be targeted or have quantifiable results.

- It is more difficult to regulate services offered by the private sector when there is a lack of clarity. In some circumstances, non-governmental organisations or local governments may be more suited to provide services.

- When customers can connect the value of a service to the price they pay for it, they are more likely to make informed decisions when purchasing complex services.

- The dissemination of information to the public and the necessity of consumer education are crucial.
- For private services to be successful, they should be less vulnerable to fraud than public ones.
- When it comes to providing public services, equity is crucial. In general, the capital owner, the customer, and the general public can all gain from privatization.

## Privatisation In India – An Inside Look

Even though there were a few rare instances of privatization in India, no firm policy decisions were made until the new economic strategy was introduced. Many state-owned enterprises (SOEs), like certain state transportation organizations, have accrued losses exceeding their capital investments. Therefore, it is vital to privatize some industries and sectors in order to ease the public's financial burden, free up more funds for development initiatives, and allow the government to focus more on key priorities.

A big step towards privatization has been taken with the adoption of the new industrial policy, which has eliminated the public sector monopoly in all but a few industries. The new programme also suggests privatizing businesses by offering shares to the public, employees, and mutual funds. In an effort to sell off public investments, the central government has been examining the portfolio of current investments.

In order to recommend the procedures for carrying out the disinvestment of stocks for particular PSUs, the Government of India established the Disinvestments Commission in August 1996. For several PSUs, the commission has recommended disinvestments at different levels.

Transferring ownership and/or administration of an enterprise from the public sector to the private sector is known as privatization, and it has become a global trend. It also refers to the State's complete or partial disengagement from a sector or industry. Opening up a sector of the economy that has been restricted to the public sector to the private sector is another aspect of privatization.

Privatization is an unavoidable historical response to the challenges brought about by the State sector's unrestrained expansion. It evolved into an essential component of economic revival even in the so-called communist nations.

Privatization could be advantageous to society in a number of ways. By relieving the State of the losses incurred by the SOEs and cutting down on the size of the bureaucracy, it would lessen the fiscal burden on the State; allow the government to absorb financial resources; improve enterprise management; promote entrepreneurship; and hasten economic development by drawing in more resources from the private sector. Increased employee and common shareholder ownership following privatization may result in increased public scrutiny of the businesses. The government may focus more on the core duties of the state thanks to privatization.

The following are significant methods of privatization:

1. The sale of equity results in the privatization of ownership, or divestiture.

2. Privatization or denationalization.

3. Contracting, wherein the government hires other businesses to manufacture and provide services.

4. Urban transport and utilities frequently use franchising, which permits the provision of certain services in predetermined geographic areas.

5. The government ceasing to provide some goods and services, leaving the private sector to handle them either entirely or in part.

6. Leases and management contracts are used to privatize management.

7. Formal or informal liquidation may take place. An organization that has undergone formal liquidation will close and sell its assets. A company that goes into informal liquidation keeps its legal status even if it suspends some or all of its operations.

Various challenges could face governments when attempting to privatize. Political parties and trade unions may be against privatization. The comparatively underdeveloped financial markets in emerging nations might occasionally make it challenging for governments to sell shares. Another issue is that governments typically wish to sell the businesses that are the least lucrative and that the private sector will not purchase for a price that suits them.

Successful privatization will only occur when specific requirements are met. There should be appropriate privatization strategies and a very clear policy. The government's dedication and political audacity are equally significant.

One of the most significant components of India's economic reforms was privatization. However, the impact of leftist parties on the UPA Government, which took office in May 2004, has caused a setback for privatization.

## Disinvestment

The Chandrashekhar Government's divestment programme, which was announced in the Interim Budget 1991–1992, called for the government to sell up to 20% of its equity in a few PSEs to institutional investors in the public sector. Broadening equity, enhancing management, increasing the availability of resources for these PSEs, and producing resources for the exchequer were all cited as goals of the policy.

The government promised to sell off a portion of its stake in a few PSEs, but the Industrial Policy Statement from July 24, 1991, did not specify how much may be sold off.

Furthermore, it did not limit disinvestment in favour of any one investor class. Disinvestment was intended to further discipline the market and improve the performance of public firms. The Budget Speech of

1991–1992, however, restored the twenty percent disinvestment cap and once more expanded the pool of eligible investors to include public sector investment institutions, mutual funds, and employees of these businesses. Additionally, the goals were changed to read as follows: "to raise resources, encourage wider public participation and promote greater accountability."

A Committee on Disinvestment in Public Sector Enterprises was established by the Indian government in 1993, and C. Rangarajan served as its head.

In 1996, the United Front Government's Common Minimum Programme aimed to thoroughly assess the public sector's non-core strategic areas and establish a Disinvestment Commission to provide advice on disinvestment-related issues, make and carry out disinvestment decisions transparently, and guarantee job security and opportunities for retraining and redeployment. Nonetheless, the policy statement made no mention of a disinvestment goal.

Strategic and Non-strategic Classification: In order to facilitate disinvestment, the government categorized the Public Sector Enterprises on March 16, 1999, into strategic and non-strategic regions.

It was decided that the following sectors would comprise the Strategic Public Sector Enterprises: atomic energy (apart from those related to nuclear power generation and applications of radiation and radio-isotopes to agriculture, medicine, and non-strategic industries); railway transport; and arms and ammunition as well as allied items of defence equipment, defence aircraft, and warships.

It was decided to classify all other public sector enterprises as non-strategic. It was decided that the government's interest would not automatically be reduced to 26% for non-strategic PSEs; instead, the process and timeline for doing so would be determined case-by-case. The following factors would be taken into account when deciding on the percentage of disinvestment, or the government's stake dropping to less than 51% or 26%: whether the industrial sector needs the public sector to be present as a countervailing force to prevent the concentration of power in private hands, and whether the industrial sector needs an appropriate regulatory mechanism to protect consumer interests prior to the privatization of public sector enterprises.

Highlights of the 2000–01 policy included the government's first declaration that it was willing to cut its stake in non-strategic PSEs to as little as 26% if necessary, a greater focus on strategic sales, the allocation of all proceeds from disinvestment and privatization to the social sector, PSE restructuring, and the retirement of public debt.

**Rangarajan Committee Recommendations**

The necessity of significant disinvestment was highlighted in the recommendations of the Report of the Committee on the Disinvestment of Shares in PSEs (Rangarajan Committee), which was submitted in April 1993. The Committee recommended that in industries specifically designated for the public sector, the amount of equity to be transferred might reach 49%. The recommendation was to maintain the target public ownership level at 26%, meaning that disinvestment could occur up to 74% in exceptional cases, such as businesses with a dominant market share or those where maintaining a distinct identity was necessary for strategic reasons. It advocated the complete divestiture of the government's stake in every other instance. Only six Schedule industries—coal and lignite; mineral oils; armaments, ammunition, and defence equipment; atomic energy; radioactive minerals; and railway transportation—were advised to have at least 51 percent of their equity held by the government.

**Disinvestment Commission**

On August 23, 1996, the Government of India established a Public Sector Disinvestment Commission in accordance with the United Front's Common Minimum Programme. The commission's general mandate was as follows:

**1** Within five to ten years, to create a comprehensive long-term disinvestment plan for the PSUs that the Core Group has referred to it.

**2** To ascertain the level of disinvestment in each PSU (total/partial indicating percentage).

**3** To assign a higher priority to the PSUs that the Core Group referred to it in relation to the overall disinvestment plan.

**4** To suggest, for each of the identified PSUs, the recommended mode(s) of disinvestment (domestic capital markets, overseas capital markets, auction, private sale to designated investors, or any other). additionally to recommend a suitable combination of the different options while keeping the state of the industry in mind.

5   To suggest a combination of primary and secondary disinvestments while keeping in mind the goals of the government, the funding needs of the relevant PSU, and the state of the market.

6   To oversee the entire sale process and make suitable judgements on the instrument, pricing, scheduling, etc.

7   To choose the financial advisors who would help with the disinvestment process for the designated PSUs.

8   To make sure that the right steps are taken to safeguard the interests of the impacted employees during the disinvestment process, including promoting employee involvement in the selling process.

The government refers units of the public sector to the Disinvestment Commission, an advisory body whose job it is to advise the government on disinvestment matters. Along with advising the government on any more disinvestment-related issues that may be specifically brought to it, the Commission will also handle any additional disinvestment-related tasks that the government may delegate to it. The Commission must also consider the interests of workers, employees, and other stakeholders in the public sector unit(s) when formulating its recommendations. The Government has the final say over the Disinvestment Commission's recommendations.

Disinvestment at different levels has been recommended

by the Commission for several PSUs (e.g., MFIL, GAIL, MTNL, CONCOR, PHL, ET&T, HVOC, HCIL, RICL, R-Ashok and U-Ashok and NALCO).

Numerous businesses, including BALCO, ITI, HTL, KIOCL, ITDC, BRPL, MFL, HCL, SCI, EIL, EPIL, HPL, IBP, NEPA, HZL, PPCL, FACT, HLL, IPCL, NFL, and SAIL, have been advised to pursue strategic sales in varying amounts.

## Globalization

The stringent economic rules that were in place up until 1991 severely restricted India's ability to integrate economically with the rest of the globe. Indian businesses mostly restricted themselves to the domestic market.

Indian businesses made very little foreign investment. But things have changed since 1991, when a new economic strategy was introduced.

In truth, globalization has recently gained popularity among Indian businesses, and many are using various tactics to grow their international operations.

According to one definition, globalization is "the growing economic interdependence of countries worldwide through increasing volume and variety of international capital flows and cross-border transactions in goods and services, as well as through the more rapid and widespread diffusion of technology."

Globalization can be evaluated on two different levels. That is, both at the macro (globalization of the world economy) and micro (globalization of the business and the firm) levels.

It goes without saying that globalizing national economies leads to globalization of the global economy. Globalization of business and globalization of economies are closely related.

**Purpose**

- The world's time and distance are rapidly decreasing due to increased financial flows, quicker communication, quicker transportation, and quicker technical advancements.

- The local markets are no longer wealthy enough. It is essential to establish production facilities abroad and do market research internationally.

- Businesses may decide to expand internationally in search of political stability, which is generally favourable in other nations.

- To acquire management expertise and technology.

- Businesses sometimes establish plants abroad in order to save expensive shipping expenses.

A few businesses have opened up shop abroad in order to be near their suppliers of raw materials and the markets where their final goods are sold. Other advancements have also added to the growing international nature of business.

- With the signing of the North American Free Trade Agreement (NAFTA), trade obstacles between the US, Canada, and Mexico will be eliminated.
- The World Trade Organization (WTO) was established to promote greater international trade.

**Aspects**

The characteristics of the current stage of globalization are as follows:

Fresh markets

- Expanding international markets for banking, insurance, and transportation services.
- New financial markets: deregulated, worldwide connected, open 24/7, with real-time action taking place remotely, and utilizing novel products like derivatives.
- The growth of mergers and acquisitions and the deregulatory treatment of antitrust legislation.
- Global brands in global consumer marketplaces.
- Fresh performers
- Global firms that combine marketing and production have a monopoly on food production.
- The World Trade Organization, the first international body with the power to compel national governments to abide with regulations
- The creation of a worldwide criminal justice system

- A thriving global network of non-governmental organizations (NGOs)
- Growing and more significant regional blocs, such as the Southern African Development Community, Mercosur, North American Free Trade Association, Association of South-East Asian Nations, and European Union
- Additional policy coordination groups: the OECD 30, G-7, G40, G22, and G77.

New guidelines and standards

Global adoption of market economic policies, more liberalized and privatized than in previous decades; expanding coverage and signatories of human rights conventions and instruments; global development goals and action agenda; global environmental conventions and agreements, including those pertaining to biodiversity, the ozone layer, the disposal of hazardous waste, desertification, and climate change; multilateral trade agreements that take on new agendas such as environmental and social conditions; new multilateral agreements, more binding on national governments than any previous

Phases of Internationalization

A company can grow from one to five distinct stages before becoming a worldwide business.

**Initial phase**

The first phase is the arm's length service operation of a primarily domestic corporation that collaborates with regional dealers and distributors to enter new international markets.

Phase two

The business assumes control of these tasks on its own in stage two.

**Phase three**

Subsequently, the domestic corporation initiates its own manufacturing, marketing, and sales in the major international markets.

Fourth phases

The corporation transitions to a full insider position in these markets in stage four, backed by a full business system that includes engineering and research and development.

At this point, the managers are expected to duplicate the hardware, systems, and operational strategies that have been so successful at home in a new setting.

Fifth Stage: During this phase, the business begins to operate on a really worldwide scale.

The following are the different approaches a company can use to transition into a global corporation:

**Exporting**

Even now, exporting is still one of the most popular ways to get into international markets.

Franchises and Licencing . A company in one nation (the licensor) grants permission to a company in another (the licensee) to utilise its intellectual property (such as patents, trademarks, copyrights, technology, technical know-how, marketing expertise, or any other particular talent) under the terms of international licencing.

A parent corporation, known as the franchisor, gives another autonomous entity, known as the franchisee, the authority to do business in a predetermined way. This is known as franchising.

## Outsourcing production

When a corporation engages in international marketing, it contracts with companies abroad to assemble or manufacture its products, but it still manages the marketing campaign.

## Contracting out management

Under a management contract, the provider assembles a team of competencies to offer the client a comprehensive service without taking on the risk or reward of ownership. If the contracting firm is granted the chance to acquire shares in the managed company within a specified timeframe, the arrangement becomes even more alluring.

## Turnkey agreements

A turnkey operation is when a seller agrees to provide a buyer with a facility that is completely furnished and prepared for use by the buyer's staff after they have received seller-provided training.

In international commerce, turnkey contracts are frequently used for the supply, construction, and commissioning of plants. Examples of such projects are steel mills, cement and fertilizer plants, oil refineries, and steel mills.

## Completely Owned Production Sites

Businesses that have a strong, long-term interest in international markets typically set up fully owned manufacturing plants there. The organization must have adequate managerial and financial resources in order to implement this strategy.

## Operations for assembly

Establishing foreign assembly facilities in specific markets may be advantageous for a company who wants many of the benefits of having manufacturing operations abroad but does not want to go that far. Starting an assembly line is like crossing the lines between manufacturing abroad and exporting.

## Partnerships

A joint venture is any kind of partnership that suggests cooperation over an extended length of time. Some examples of cooperative foreign operations are:

In an enterprise, joint ownership and management

Agreements for franchising and licencing.

Outsourcing production

Contracts for management

Acquisitions and mergers

Acquisitions and mergers (M&A) have been a key component of both expansion and market entry strategies.

Numerous Indian enterprises have also employed this approach to market penetration.

**Strategic partnership**

By building alliances with future or current rivals in key markets rather than engaging in direct competition, this strategy aims to strengthen the company's long-term competitive advantage. Another tactic occasionally employed to enter a market is a strategic alliance. One way for a company to enter a foreign market is by partnering with another company operating there.

**Counter-exchange**

Counter commerce encompasses a range of non-traditional international trade methods that involve the exchange of goods, either directly or indirectly, with the aim of eliminating the need for monetary exchanges. Counter trade is a type of international trade in which certain export and import transactions are directly related to one another and where commodities are exported in lieu of cash payments to cover the cost of imports.

**Advantages of globalization**

A few key justifications for globalization are as follows:

- Productivity increases quicker when nations create commodities and services in which they have a competitive advantage;
- Living standards can rise more quickly.

- Since imports and global competition keep prices in check, inflation is less likely to impede economic growth

**Disadvantages of globalization**

The cases against globalization are as follows:

- Production moves abroad or imports have resulted in millions of job losses. Millions of people dread losing their jobs, especially in those companies that are under pressure from competitors. The majority find new positions that pay less.

- Employers frequently threaten to export employment if workers don't agree to wage reduction demands.

- White-collar jobs and services are becoming more and more susceptible to operations shifting overseas.

- When businesses establish sophisticated factories in low-wage nations, where the workers are just as productive as those in the United States, the workers may lose their comparative advantage.

The growth of international trade between 1950 and 1970 gave rise to the globalisation process in the 1950s. Trade expanded as more regional organizations, such as the EU and NAFTA, emerged, but they also had problems of their own that needed to be fixed. Thus, wealthy economies begged for globalization in order to gain from its expansion of international markets. In 1950, global exports brought in $61 billion; by 1970, they had risen to $315 billion, and by 2010, they had reached $14,855 billion. The current value of global exports is $17,779.

Globalization in India: In July 1980, the government led by Mrs. Gandhi released a revised Industrial Policy Statement. The policy's direction changed to promote "liberalisation" and "export-promotion," although this transition was only acknowledged in the middle of the 1980s. A unique endeavour to promote and quicken industrial growth was highlighted in the sixth plan statement under the heading "New Industrial Growth with Direct Measures for Poverty eradications." 'Industrial Growth and Liberalization' was the Seventh Five Year Plan's development plan. In addition, a number of crises, including the BOP crisis of the 1980s, the oil shock, the economy's sluggish growth, India's credit rating downgrade, gold pledges overseas, and others, hampered the country's economic advancement.

As a result, the circumstances of 1990–1991 forced India to embrace the globalization process and implement a structural adjustment project. Under the leadership of Manmonhan Singh, the Finance Minister at the time, and the present Prime Minister, P V Narasimha Rao, the country began a new era of economic reforms in 1991 (1991-95). Call it the globalization age, but the Indian economy saw a profound break from its socialist beliefs for the first time.

**Steps towards Globalization-**

Import liberalization: import restrictions via licence were eliminated. Now, it was simple to import any capital goods, raw materials, or intermediate goods with just the payment of customs duties. In 1995, all quantitative limitations for consumer goods were lifted. Peak customs tax was gradually lowered from 300% to 150% by 1991, then to 85% in 1993, and finally to 12.5% in 2006 in an effort to liberalize imports. In 1999, additional modifications were implemented to comply with TRIPS, including the establishment of exclusive marketing rights.

Import of Gold and Silver- it was made free and further it was freed from any commission charged for it.

Exchange rate set by the market: by making currency completely convertible, it permitted the market to set its own exchange rates on the global stage without the need for government interference. Exchange control was gradually removed. On July 1st and 3, 991, the Indian government adjusted the rupee's currency rate in two steps, decreasing it by 18–19%. The market determined exchange rate was established in 1993 when the exchange rate was moved to a unified exchange rate system.

Rupee convertibility: A change was made to the rupee's convertibility on the BOP on current account. By exchanging the rupee for dollars at the foreign exchange market, importers can now obtain the desired amount of foreign exchange. Exporters were now able to sell their foreign exchange profits on the foreign exchange market directly.

Liberalization of Foreign Investments and Portfolio Foreign Investments: Both direct and portfolio foreign investments were made more permissible by the NEP. Up to 51% of the entire equity capital of the companies in 34 priority industries could be approved automatically by FDI without the need for previous government approval.

The government increased the maximum percentage of foreign equity participation to 74% in 1996.

A number of industries were made available to the private sector once limits on industrial licencing were lifted. Subject to SEBI registration and RBI permission, NRIs were permitted to invest up to 100% in high priority industries, as well as up to 100% in trading houses, export houses, hospitals, and sick industries. Foreign institutional investors, or FIIs, were also permitted to invest in the Indian capital market. All manufacturing activity in SEZs are eligible for 100% of FDIs under the automatic route. Additionally, 100% FDI is allowed in the mass transit system, town ship development, hotel and tourism, pharma, and airport industries. FDI in private banks has increased to 74% and FDI in private airlines to 49%.

To do away with restrictions on foreign equity corporations, the Foreign Exchange Regulation Act (FERA) was superseded by the Foreign Exchange Management Act (FEMA). India attracted foreign portfolio investment through a combination of push and pull factors.

**Effects of Globalization-**

1. In 1995, it caused a significant increase in foreign exchange to reach over 20 USD billion. From $1.1 billion in 1991 to $304.8 billion in 2011 and finally to $295.6 billion by the end of December 2012, the foreign exchange reserves stock increased.

2. Exports rose by more than 17% in 1993–1994 as a result of exporters' favourable reactions to the policy changes. Although they increased throughout this time, imports had little impact on the balance of payments.

3. The liberalization programme did make our nation more independent.

4. The 1994–1995 current account deficit was predicted to be less than 0.5%. The amount of external debt was lowered to under $1 billion.

5. Despite the implementation of full convertibility on both the trade account and the current account, the rupee's exchange rate stayed stable. Legal avenues were used to bring in foreign exchange.

6. The creation of job possibilities.

7. There was a return of international trust in India.

8. The market and consumerism are expanding.

9. Increased the effectiveness of the banking, insurance, and financial sectors by allowing foreign money, banks, and insurance corporations to operate there.

**Foreign Capital**

In path of economic development, the majority of nations in the world were somewhat dependent on foreign finance. However, the level of dependence varied depending on a number of factors, including the ability to mobilize domestic resources, the status of the domestic economy in terms of technological advancement, the stance taken by the various governments, etc. However, it is an undeniable reality that foreign capital plays a significant role in the process of industrialization and economic expansion.

## Need of foreign capital

One of the following factors may cause a developing nation like India to require foreign capital:

- There is not enough domestic capital to support economic expansion.

- Domestic capital and entrepreneurship may not flow into particular industrial lines due to a lack of experience.

- Potential savings might exist in a developing nation like India, but they might only materialize at a more advanced stage of economic development.

- Projects that are desperately needed for economic development may be difficult to finance with domestic funds; also, foreign capital provides other scarce productive factors, like technological know-how, commercial experience, and information.

## Types of Foreign Investment

The many types of foreign investments include:

Direct Foreign Investment: Direct investments from overseas might bring money into India.

International Cooperation

Three kind of international collaborations exist: cooperative efforts between private entities, foreign corporations and the Indian government, and foreign governments and the Indian government.

## Loans between governments

Direct loans and grants between governments have become more common after the Second World War.

India has mostly benefited from loans from international institutions such as the World Bank, Asian Development Bank (ADB), Aid India Consortium, and International Monetary Fund (IMF).

Export credit organisations such as the US Export-Im Bank, the Japanese Exim Bank, and the UK's ECGC, among others, use external commercial borrowing (ECB) to secure commercial borrowing from the capital market.

In 1991, the Indian government liberalised its laws governing foreign investment, allowing for the automatic acceptance of up to 51 percent equity foreign ownership in 34 industries. In addition, the Foreign Investment Promotion Board (FIPB) was established to handle applications that did not qualify for automatic approval. In order to promote direct foreign investment, portfolio investment, NRI investment, and other forms of investment, several other initiatives were implemented in 1992–1993.

## Overseas cooperation

The national policy towards foreign capital did acknowledge the need for foreign capital during the early planning era, but it chose not to give it a dominating position. As a result, foreign partnerships had to give the Indian counterpart a majority stake and maintain their equity below the 49% cap.

Furthermore, international cooperation was to be allowed in important areas, particularly in those where our skills were still developing.

However, generally speaking, our approach to international partnerships remained constrictive and biased. As a result, 2,475 international collaborations were authorised between 1961 and 1970, while 3, 041 collaborations were sanctioned between 1971 and 1980.

The government did not ease its stance on international cooperation until the 1980s. This was done especially for investors from developing nations that export oil and have clearly specified package exemptions. The January 1983 release of the Technology Policy Statement (TPS) came next. The policy's goal was to import technology while making sure it was of the newest generation suitable for the nation's needs and resources.

**Nation's foreign investments**

Technical partnerships were permitted subject to certain financial requirements, such as royalties, lump sum payments, or a mix of the two. Due to these relaxations, there was an increase in foreign direct investment in US, which led to a record number of approvals during the 1981–1990 decade (7,436), representing a total investment of Rs. 1, 274 crores.

An examination of foreign partnership by country shows that the United States led the pack, receiving investments of around Rs. 322.7 crores. This accounted for 1/4 of the 91 approvals for overseas collaborations. The Federal Republic of Germany (17.2%), Japan, the United Kingdom, Italy, France, and Switzerland came next. Of all allowed foreign investment, five countries accounted for roughly 63%: the United States, West Germany, Japan, the United Kingdom, and Italy. Even Non-Resident Indians (NRIs) made a contribution of approximately Rs. 113 crores, or 8.9% of the total amount invested.

**Investing abroad through industries**

Electrical and electronic (including telecommunications) accounted for 22% of all permits, showing the highest priority to this sector, followed by industrial equipment (15.5%), according to an industry-wise analysis of foreign collaboration permissions. The relevance of foreign cooperation in chemicals (apart from fertilizers) was ranked third. Generally speaking, it may be said that 70% of all approvals were granted to the priority industry. It suggests that at the time, the nation's overall attitude towards foreign money was about in line with the approvals granted for international cooperation.

Technical and financial cooperation

**There are two categories of foreign partnerships:**
- Financial approvals involving stock capital of an existing or new company;

- Technical approvals including payments for technology.

  Larger projects above these caps are approved by the Cabinet Committee on Foreign Investment (CCFI), although the Industry Ministry approves projects up to Rs. 600 crores on the Foreign Investment Promotion Board's (FIPB) advice.

- The percentage of financial cooperation was just 20.1% in 1981–1985, but it increased to 28.8% in 1985–1990 and then dramatically to 72% in 1991–1997.

- In August 1998, the approved investment amount had risen significantly from Rs. 899 crores in 1985–1990 to Rs. 1,73,510 crores.

It is evident that throughout the post-liberalization phase, financial approvals replace technical clearances. In contrast to the previous phase, the government has managed to draw in more foreign investment in the post-liberalization phase.

**Taking over and foreign collaborations**

Indian business owners appear to have less negotiating leverage, and multinational corporations (TNCs) now own well-known Indian brands. It is important to note that acquisitions do not result in the addition of additional production capacity. On the other hand, there will probably be a greater outflow of foreign currency. Transferring advanced technology has not been the primary focus of international partnerships.

A Few Latest Acquisitions

- An attempt was made by ICI (UK) to acquire Asian paints.
- Tomco was taken up by Hindustan lever.
- Premier Automobiles gave Peugeot control of two of its plants.
- Lakme's brand is transferred to a 50:50 joint venture with the Levers; TVS Suzuki acquires Hero Honda; TVS Whirlpool is acquired by Whirlpool; and Suzuki attempts to acquire a majority stake in Maruti Udyog.
- Bridgestone upped its share in the joint venture with ACC from 51% to 74%.
- Bausch & Lomb is boosting its stake to 69% in an Indian partnership.
- Henkel raising its ownership stake to 70%.
- Blue Star surpassed both Hewlett Packard India and Motorola Blue Star.
- Shriram's ownership stake in Shriram Honda Power was decreased.

Upon transferring the units, the Indian partners did not carry any funds or marketing connections with them.

## Foreign Trade Policy In India

India's foreign trade policy is a framework established by the government to regulate and promote international trade. The policy aims to enhance exports, improve trade relations, and boost the overall economic growth of the country.

## Objectives of India's Foreign Trade Policy

### 1 Boost Exports:

Increase the volume and value of goods and services exported from India.

Enhance global competitiveness of Indian products.

### 2 Generate Employment:

Create job opportunities through increased production and export activities.

### 3 Diversify Export Markets:

Reduce dependency on a few markets by exploring new trade destinations.

### 4 Promote Value Addition:

Encourage the export of high-value and technologically advanced products.

### 5 Improve Trade Balance:

Reduce the trade deficit by increasing exports and managing imports.

## Key Components of India's Foreign Trade Policy

### 1 Export Promotion Schemes:

**Merchandise Exports from India Scheme (MEIS):** Provides incentives to exporters of goods to offset infrastructural inefficiencies and associated costs.

**Service Exports from India Scheme (SEIS):** Rewards exporters of notified services to promote the export of services.

## 2 Duty Exemption/Remission Schemes:

**Advance Authorization Scheme:** Allows duty-free import of inputs for export production.

**Duty Drawback Scheme:** Refunds the customs duties paid on imported inputs used in the manufacture of exported goods.

## 3 Export Oriented Units (EOUs) and Special Economic Zones (SEZs):

**EOUs:** Units that export their entire production and benefit from duty exemptions and other incentives.

**SEZs:** Designated areas with more liberal economic laws to promote exports, featuring tax benefits, infrastructural support, and simplified procedures.

## 4 Trade Infrastructure for Export Scheme (TIES):

Aims to enhance export infrastructure by developing logistics, warehousing, and quality testing facilities.

## 5 Export Credit and Guarantee:

**Export Credit Guarantee Corporation (ECGC):** Provides insurance cover to exporters against payment risks.

**Interest Equalization Scheme:** Offers interest subsidy on pre- and post-shipment rupee export credit to make Indian exports competitive.

## Recent Developments and Initiatives

### 1 Digital Initiatives:

**e-Trade:** Streamlining export-import documentation and procedures through digital platforms to reduce transaction costs and time.

**Digital Certificates of Origin:** Implementation of electronic certificates to simplify trade processes.

### 2 Focus on New Markets:

Initiatives to explore and enter new and emerging markets in Africa, Latin America, and Southeast Asia to diversify export destinations.

### 3 Quality and Standards:

Emphasis on adhering to international quality standards and certifications to enhance the credibility and marketability of Indian products.

### 4 Atmanirbhar Bharat (Self-Reliant India):

Promoting self-reliance in manufacturing to reduce import dependency and increase export capacity.

### 5 Trade Agreements:

Engaging in bilateral and multilateral trade agreements to facilitate easier market access for Indian goods and services.

# Questions

| Question | Option 1 | Option 2 | Option 3 | Option 4 | Answer |
|---|---|---|---|---|---|
| Locate the word that is concerned with the withdrawal of State from an industry or sector, partially or fully | Liberalization | Modernization | Privatization | Globalization | 3 |
| Identify the date on which The Govt. of India constituted a Public Sector Disinvestment commission | 15-Mar-91 | 23 Aug 1996 | 23 Sept.1993 | 06-May-94 | 2 |
| Indicate the type of securities those are | Pvt. Securities | Govt. securities | Initial securities | None of these | 2 |

| | | | | | |
|---|---|---|---|---|---|
| bought and sold in open market operation | | | | | |
| Predict the Bill that is concerned with the tax proposals of the Budget | Cash Bill | Finance Bill | State Bill | None of these | 2 |
| Indicate the item of the budget that is concerned with the current expenditure of Govt. on administration | Capital expenditure | Revenue expenditure | Deferred expenditure | None of these | 2 |
| Predict the full form of CSR | Company Social Responsibility | Corporate Social Rights | Corporate Social Responsibility | Company Social Rights | 3 |

| Indicate the benefit that is derived from competitive rivalry | Price war | Differentiation | Alliances | Higher marketing budgets | 2 |
|---|---|---|---|---|---|
| Predict the proper acronym of PESTLE | Political, environmental, technological, legal, and environmental | Political, environmental, shareholding, technological, logistical, and e-marketing | Political, economic, social, technological, legal, and environmental | Political, environmental, societal, technological, learning, and e-marketing | 3 |
| Identify the nature of activity enumerated in Corporate governance | External regulation | Self-regulation | Government control | Charitable action | 2 |
| Predict the strategy that organisations need to adopt | Relocation strategy | Creation of subsidiaries | Competitive strategy | Collusion | 3 |

| | | | | | |
|---|---|---|---|---|---|
| to overcome competition | | | | | |
| Select the process of the sale of substandard and hazardous goods under defined conditions. | Restrictive Trade Practice | Unfair Trade Practice | MRTP | None of these | 2 |

---

Estimate implications of globalization on Indian economy.

Evaluate role of Government of India in managing balance of payments.

Estimate the success of a business enterprise is significantly influenced by its environment.

Estimate the effects of economic changes those were initiated by the Government under the Industrial Policy, 1991.

# Chapter 5
# International Organizations

**CHAPTER CONTENT**

GATT

WTO

IMF

World Bank

**GATT**

During the 1930s and the Second World War, a system of strict and widespread trade restrictions was observed by the global community. The United States and its allies worked to provide the framework and circumstances for free commerce in Western Europe following the war. 53 nations endorsed an ITO charter during the 1948 UN Conference on Trade and Employment in Havana. However, the US Congress was unable to ratify the Havana Charter, therefore the idea was dropped.

53 countries in all signed the charter establishing it. 23 countries decided to accept a comprehensive tariff agreement in exchange for trade concessions in Geneva,

which resulted in the creation of GATT on January 1st, 1948. India was the founder member of GATT.

**Objectives of GATT-**

To adhere to the most-favorable-nation (MFN) principle without reservation.

To conduct business according to the principles of openness, reciprocity, and nondiscrimination.

The use of tariffs to protect domestic industries.

To use international talks to liberalize tariff and non-tariff measures. Multilateral trade talks, consultation, conciliation, dispute resolution, and waivers for extraordinary circumstances were all outlined in the agreement.

Tariff Negotiations and Tariff Reduction: An entrenched clause in the GATT aimed to stabilise the tariffs of its member nations. All concessions made by contracting parties as a result of GATT talks are required to be recorded in a "Schedule of Concessions," according to Article II of the GATT. It promoted regular talks between the contractual parties to significantly lower the import tariff rates. The different needs of the contracting parties had to be taken into consideration throughout the reciprocal and mutually beneficial tariff reduction talks. The LDCs were granted a certain amount of tariff protection under the GATT due to their unique industrial development requirements and as a means of generating income.

Subsidies and Counter-Veiling Duties: The GATT acknowledged that subsidies were a better option than tariffs. In the 1970s, the GATT Tokyo Round determined that a code of conduct pertaining to subsidies was required. The industrialised nations decided to outright forbid export subsidies for goods that are produced. This requirement did not apply to LDCs.

## WTO – Status

It serves as the institutional and legal basis for multilateral commerce. It is a permanent organisation established by an international treaty that has been approved by the national and state legislatures of all participating nations. It comprises of 500 pages of individual agreements made at the Uruguay round of discussions and a document on general agreement with 38 item codes.

### Objectives:

To raise the living standards of citizens in the participating nations.

To guarantee both a wide rise in effective demand and full employment.

To increase trade and manufacture of commodities.

To boost the exchange of services.

To guarantee the best possible use of global resources.

### Functions:

To put into effect the directives and clauses pertaining to the trade policy review process. to give member nations a forum to choose their future trade and tariff policies.

To offer resources for the administration, execution, and functioning of bilateral and multilateral agreements related to global commerce.

To oversee the procedures and guidelines pertaining to conflict resolution.

**Structure**

Headquartered in Geneva, the WTO secretariat employs over 600 people and is led by a Director-General. The Ministerial Council appoints the Director-General for a four-year tenure. Four of his deputies are from various member nations.

**The Essential Elements and Characteristics of WTO**

Non-Discrimination: The most favoured nation (MFN) designation will be accorded to all trading partners, meaning that each WTO member state will treat every other member state equally as the most favoured nation engaging in trade. Trademarks, copyrights, patents, and foreign goods and services must all be treated in the same way as domestic ones.

Free Trade: Through talks, the WTO seeks to advance free trade between countries. The WTO has pushed for a gradual liberalisation of trade by lowering tariffs and doing away with quantitative import limits for its member nations.

Stability in the Trading System: Member states are bound by WTO accords to refrain from arbitrary tariff and non-tariff trade barrier increases. This gives the trading system consistency and predictability.

Multilateral Trading System: The primary objective of the World Trade Organisation (WTO) is to create an equitable and just multilateral system of international trade in which developed, developing, and least developed countries alike have equal access to foreign markets for their products. Additionally, the organisation aims to remove unfair trade barriers and government support for exports by different countries.

## International Monetary Fund

After abolition of The General Agreement on Tariffs and Trade (GATT) the IMF and the IBRD were established.

The foundation of the global monetary system was established by the IMF's Articles of Agreement. Although the IMF officially came into being on December 27, 1945, when 29 countries signed its Articles of Agreement (its charter), financial operations began on March 1, 1947.

## Objectives:

The six objectives outlined in Article 1 of the Articles of Agreement (AGA) justify the establishment of the IMF.

The major functions of the IMF:

It performs the duties of a short-term lending institution.

It offers the tools necessary to regulate exchange rates in a systematic manner.

It serves as a repository for all of the member nations' currencies, from which a borrower country can obtain foreign money.

It functions somewhat like a foreign exchange lending institution. But only for financing current transactions—not capital transactions—does it offer loans.

It also offers equipment for occasionally changing a member nation's currency's par value. By doing this, it seeks to facilitate a systematic change in exchange rates that will enhance the member nations' long-term position in terms of their balance of payments. Additionally, it offers equipment for global consultations.

The oversight of the global monetary system is the IMF's primary duty. These include lending money to member nations even when they have brief imbalances in their balance of payments, keeping an eye on member nations' monetary and exchange rate policies, and making policy suggestions. It should be mentioned that the IMF can perform all three of these roles. They are the following: financial, regulatory, and consulting roles.

**Special Drawing Rights**

Paper gold is another name for Special Drawing Rights. The IMF established the SDR as an international reserve asset in 1969 to augment the official reserves of its member nations. The IMF introduced SDRs in 1969 as a reaction to the Triffin Paradox. An economic theory called the Triffin Dilemma, or Triffin paradox, emphasises the inherent tension between a nation's currency's local and international functions, especially when it comes to a global reserve currency. The economist Robert Triffin, an American who was born in Belgium, first described the conundrum in the 1960s.

The nation whose currency acts as the world's reserve currency is faced with competing goals, according to the Triffin Dilemma. On the one hand, because other nations retain its currency for transnational transactions, reserves, and investments, it must supply enough of it to meet demand worldwide. To do this, trade imbalances must be maintained throughout time in order to supply the global financial system with enough liquidity.

However, in order to guarantee the stability and value of the currency, the nation must continue to have faith in it. To do this, trade surpluses must normally be maintained in order to increase foreign reserves and keep a positive balance of payments. But chasing trade surpluses runs counter to the objective of producing enough money to meet demand everywhere.

The problem stems from the principal global reserve currency issuer's sometimes conflicting obligation to satisfy both home and foreign demands. A nation may incur unmanageable foreign liabilities and lose trust in the value of its currency if it adopts policies, such as running trade deficits, to meet the world's demand for its currency. On the other hand, if it prioritizes preserving trade surpluses over maintaining currency credibility, this may lead to a dearth of the world's reserve currency, which would limit global liquidity.

Triffin contended that this conundrum produces an inherent instability in the international monetary system. The interests of the global economy and the issuing nation may not coincide when one country's currency serves as the worldwide reserve, which could result in financial crises and disruptions.

During the Bretton Woods system, which was in place from the end of World War II until the early 1970s, the Triffin Dilemma gained notoriety. Under this arrangement, the US dollar functioned as the world's reserve currency, and the US faced growing difficulties in balancing the competing demands of currency stability and global liquidity. In the end, the system broke down in 1971 when the United States stopped the dollar's convertibility into gold.

The international monetary system has changed since then, but the US dollar has remained the primary reserve currency for the world. No other currency has taken its position. Nonetheless, the Triffin Dilemma remains pertinent in debates about the longevity and stability of the world monetary system, particularly in view of the growing significance of developing nations and the possibility of the emergence of substitute reserve currencies.

According to the Triffin Paradox, countries' confidence in the US government's ability to convert US dollars into gold decreased with the amount of US dollars used as a base reserve currency. The initial idea was that SDRs would take the place of the US dollar as the world's monetary reserve currency, so resolving the Triffin Paradox, while the world was still operating under the Bretton Woods system. A few years after Bretton Woods collapsed, the idea of an SDR became firmly established. The U.S. dollar, the British pound, the Japanese yen, and the euro are the four major currencies that make up the value of an SDR today, but they are not equal in value. US dollars are used to quote SDRs.

The SDR plan is that it will resemble gold paper. SDR had a fixed value in gold. The member nations were required to preserve the fixed value of the SDR, which was set at 35 an ounce, or 0.888671 grammes of pure gold at the official rate of the time. One SDR was equal to one US dollar.

## World Bank

There are two entities that make up the World Bank: 1. The International Development Association (IDA), which was established in 1960; 2. The International Bank for Reconstruction and Development (IBRD), which was formerly the World Bank itself.

The Bank highlights the following for all of its clients:

1. Investing in people, especially in basic health and education;

2. Emphasizing social development, governance, and institution-building as the primary components of poverty alleviation;

3. Fortifying government capacity to provide quality services with increased efficiency and transparency;

4. Preserving the environment;

5. Fostering and promoting the growth of private enterprises and long-term planning. It is the World Bank's policy to lend money for projects, not to

cover trade deficits. There must be a plausible chance that these loans will be repaid.

The IDA was established to provide a different kind of financing. Interest-free IDA loans are available for several decades, with a ten-year grace period before the loan recipient nation is required to start loan repayment. A common term for these loans is "soft loans." It offers the following types of loans: (i) project loans, (ii) sectorial loans, and (iii) loans for structural adjustment. The international capital markets have been a source of funding for the IBRD's development operations since it first issued bonds in 1947. The World Bank issues bonds on an annual average of roughly $25 billion. Due to their backing by the combined capital of the member nations and the sovereign guarantees of the borrowers, these bonds have been assigned a AAA rating, the highest possible rating. The World Bank is able to borrow money at comparatively low interest rates thanks to its AAA credit rating. Due to their generally extremely low credit ratings, this offers developing nations an alternative, more affordable source of borrowing.

The Bank's stated goal now is to assist nations in reducing poverty by promoting economic growth and a favorable business climate. They highlight the following five elements:

1. Building Capacity
2. Infrastructure development, which includes the establishment of legal frameworks that support enterprise and safeguard private property rights.

3. The creation of financial institutions
4. Fighting the corruption
5. Studies, advice, and instruction

It provides loans of two primary types: loans for development policies and loans for investments. While development policy loans assist institutional and policy reforms, investment loans fund initiatives related to social and economic development.

In addition, the Bank awards funds for the following purposes: debt relief; fighting HIV/AIDS; providing support to civil society organizations; improving sanitation and water quality; and environmental activities.

**Objectives of the Bank**

To give member nations long-term funding for economic development and rehabilitation.

To encourage capital investment through the following channels in member nations.

To offer assurance for capital investments or private loans.

Each member nation appoints one Governor and one Alternative Governor to the board for a period of five years. Each governor has a vote that is based on the amount of money the government he represents contributes. Six of the 21 members of the Board of Executive Directors are appointed by the six largest shareholders, which are the United States, the United Kingdom, West Germany, France, Japan, and India. The remaining nations elect the remaining fifteen members.

To continue the daily operations of the bank, the board of executive directors convenes once a month. The Board of Executive Directors appoints the bank's president. He is the Bank's chief executive officer.

## Questions

| Question | Option 1 | Option 2 | Option 3 | Option 4 | Answer |
|---|---|---|---|---|---|
| Indicate the nature of activity enumerated in Corporate governance | External regulation | Self-regulation | Government control | Charitable action | 2 |
| Select the strategy that organisations need to adopt to overcome competition | Relocation strategy | Creation of subsidiaries | Competitive strategy | Collusion | 3 |
| Predict the process of the sale of substandard and hazardous goods under | Restrictive Trade Practice | Unfair Trade Practice | MRTP | None of these | 2 |

| | | | | | |
|---|---|---|---|---|---|
| defined conditions. | | | | | |
| Select the other organization other than IMF that consists The Bretton Wood Twins. | World Bank | IMF | ADB | None of these | 1 |
| Predict the geographical area where the countries come in OPEC | South East | Western Europe | Middle East | West Africa | 3 |
| Select the rate at which RBI borrows money from commercial bank | Repo Rate | Market rate of Interest | Inflation rate. | Reverse Repo rate | 4 |
| Indicate the nature of Indian Economy | Export Substitution | Import Promotion | Export Promotion | Import Substitution | 4 |

| | | | | | |
|---|---|---|---|---|---|
| prior to the 1990 | | | | | |
| Select the Central Monetary Authority of USA | International Monetary Fund | Reserve Bank | Bank of England | Federal Reserve | 4 |
| Predict the chairperson of NITI Ayyog | Home Minister | Finance Minister | Prime Minister | Chief Minister | 3 |
| Predict the rate at which commercial bank borrows money from RBI | Repo Rate | Market rate of Interest | Inflation rate | Nominal rate | 1 |
| Select the organization that does HR planning at the National Level | Consultants | Managers | Council | Government | 4 |
| Indicate the international organization that is | United Nations Organisation | UNESCO | World Health Organisation | International Labour Organisation | 4 |

| | | | | | |
|---|---|---|---|---|---|
| directly related to industrial relations at international level | | | | | |
| Identify the factors that influence consumer buying behavior | Cultural and social factors | Personal factors | Both a and b | Demographic Factors | 3 |
| Predict the other organization other than IMF that consists The Bretton Wood Twins. | World Bank | IMF | ADB | None of these | 1 |
| Indicate the geographical area where the countries come in OPEC | South East | Western Europe | Middle East | West Africa | 3 |

| |
|---|
| Explain the term 'Balance of Payments.' |
| Interpret globalization. |
| Evaluate objectives of World Bank. |
| Estimate objectives of WTO. |
| Explain Balance of Trade components. |
| Explain Balance of Payment components. |
| Evaluate effects of positive Balance of Trade. |
| Evaluate effects of negative Balance of Trade. |
| Evaluate effects of positive Balance of Payment. |
| Evaluate effects of negative Balance of Trade. |

# Chapter 6
# Human Resource Development And Sustainable Development

**CHAPTER CONTENT**

HRM

Human Resource Planning

Training and Development

HR Accounting and Audit

Sustainable Development

## Human Resource Management

### Characteristics

The following aspects of human resource management (HRM) can be recognized based on defection analyses.

1. People-Oriented: HRM is focused with helping staff members achieve objectives as individuals and as a group. It also addresses the social, emotional, and behavioural components of the workforce. It is the process of uniting individuals and groups to achieve each other's objectives.

2. Human resource management is a comprehensive function that addresses all personnel levels and classifications. It covers employees as well as managers, officers, supervisors, and other staff members. Both organized and unorganized workers are covered. It is applicable to workers in all kinds of global organizations.

3. Individual-focused: Every employee is treated as an individual under human resource management in order to provide services that support employee development and happiness. Put another way, it's about developing human resources, which includes knowledge, competence, skill, and potential, as well as reaching and surpassing employee objectives.

4. Staff Function: In an organization, staff managers are in charge of human resource management, which falls within the purview of all line managers. Although they don't produce or sell products, human resource managers help businesses succeed and expand by offering operational departments advice on human resources-related issues.

5. All forms of functional management, including production, marketing, and financial management, are influenced by human resource management, which is the primary sub function of an organization. Every manager has some involvement in the human resources department. In an organization, it is the duty of staff managers as well as all line managers.

6. Difficult Function: Because people are dynamic, managing human resources is a difficult job. To

achieve set goals, human resource management seeks to obtain the unwavering cooperation of every employee. To achieve set goals, human resource management seeks to guarantee the unconditional cooperation of every employee.

7. Development-oriented: Individual employee objectives include opportunities for growth, pride, status, recognition, difficult work, high pay, appealing benefits, and job stability. The goal of human resource management is to help people reach their full potential so they may contribute their best efforts to the company and get the most joy from their employment.

## HRM Process

HRM is a procedure made up of four steps.

(i) Purchasing human capital.

(ii) The advancement of human capital.

(iii) Human resource motivation and

(iv) Keeping up with human resources.

## Functions of HRM

(i) Acquisition Function: The acquisition process focuses on locating and hiring individuals with the kind and caliber of human resources needed to meet corporate goals. Planning is when the acquisition function starts. Additionally, it addresses tasks like internal mobility, recruitment, placement, selection, induction, and job analysis as well as human resource planning.

(ii) Development Function: The process of enhancing, molding, and altering knowledge, aptitude, creative ability, and values is known as the development function. Three dimensions can be used to view the development function:

a) Employee training: The process of teaching staff members' technical and operational skills and information is known as training. It also involves employees' attitudes shifting.

b) Management development: Improving an executive's conceptual skills and gaining new knowledge are the main goals of management development. It is the process of creating and implementing appropriate executive development courses to help staff members improve their managerial and interpersonal skills.

c) Career Development: The ongoing endeavor to align with the long-term needs of both individuals and organizations is known as career development. Effectively developed human resources should result in knowledgeable staff members who possess the most recent skills and expertise.

(iii) Motivation Function: The motivation function starts with the understanding that every person is different and that motivational strategies should be tailored to meet those needs. It is a branch of management that deals with putting employees in a work environment that inspires them to collaborate effectively and with economic, psychological, and social fulfilment.

**(iv) Maintenance Function:** This part of the job involves making sure that workers have the working.

conditions they consider essential to upholding their loyalty to the company. The maintenance function's goal is to hold onto employees who are delivering excellent work. This necessitates that the company offer healthy and safe working environments as well as positive labour relations. Effective execution of these tasks should result in competent workers who are dedicated to the company and happy in their positions.

HRM Model: There has been a fair amount of consensus among HRM experts in recent years over the definition of the discipline of HRM. Nine human resource areas are identified under the American Society for Training and Development (ASTD) model:

1. Education and Training
2. Development of Organizations
3. Structure / Work Design
4. Planning for Human Resources
5. Choosing and Assigning Personnel
6. Information Systems and Personnel Research
7. Remuneration and Benefits
8. Workers' Aid
9. Labour Relations in Unions.

Education and Training

To survive and achieve shared objectives, organizations and individuals must grow and change at the same time.

One of the core operational facets of human resource management is the specialized role of employee training. Employee knowledge, skills, behaviour, aptitude, and attitude towards the demands of the position and the company are all enhanced, changed, and moulded by training. Training fills in the gaps between an employee's current specifications and the demands of their job.

The methodical process of growth and development known as "management development" helps managers hone their managerial skills. It is an organized endeavour to raise managerial performance, either now or in the future.

**Development of Organizations**

With a methodical and well-planned change effort, management may effectively address change's problems. The contemporary method for managing change and developing human resources is organization development. Organization development (OD) focuses on people dimensions like norms, values, attitudes, relationships, organizational climate, etc. Organization development (OD) is defined by Dale S. Beach as "a complex educational strategy designed to increase organizational effectiveness and wealth through planned intervention by a consultant using theory and techniques of applied behavioural science." The overall goals of OD initiatives are to increase employee job satisfaction and organizational effectiveness. These goals can be fulfilled by fostering each employee's personal development and humanizing the companies.

Job/Organization Design: Organizational structure is the focus of organization design. Its goal is to analyze roles and relationships in order to explicitly organize group activity towards particular goals. Units and positions comprise the organizational structure that is developed as a result of the design process. These units and roles have relationships that involve the use of authority and the sharing of information.

Planning for Human Resources

The process of evaluating an organization's needs for human resources in relation to its goals and creating strategies to guarantee the employment of a skilled, reliable workforce is known as human resource planning.

## Choosing and Assigning Personnel

The management must choose the best candidate at the correct moment after determining where to find human resources, looking for potential hires, and encouraging them to apply for positions. Establishing a sound organizational structure is crucial, but placing the appropriate people in the proper positions is even more crucial. Staffing consists of the following sub-functions:

(i) Hiring or receiving applications for positions as they become available.

(ii) Choosing the most competent applicant from among those who apply for positions.

(iii) Promotions and transfers

(iv) Providing additional training to individuals who require it in order to do their jobs well or to be eligible for promotions.

The significance and necessity of adequate staffing: Appropriate and effective staffing has several benefits. These are listed in the following order:

(i) It facilitates the identification of skilled and capable employees and their advancement up the corporate ladder.

(ii) By placing the appropriate guy in the proper task, it guarantees higher production.

(iii) By disclosing any workforce shortages in advance, it helps to prevent an abrupt interruption of an enterprise's production run.

(iv) It aids in preventing employee underutilization due to overscheduling, which raises labour costs and reduces profit margins.

(v) In the case of an unforeseen turnover, it gives management the knowledge they need for the internal succession of managing staff.

**Recruitment And Selection**

Flippo defines recruitment as the process of looking for potential employees and motivating and pushing them to submit applications for positions within a company.

"Recruiting is the process of identifying possible candidates for current or upcoming organisational vacancies," according to Mamoria.

Hence, the process of generating applications or candidates for particular roles is known as recruiting. It's a connecting activity that brings together job seekers and those who already have jobs. Therefore, recruiting is the process of looking for potential employees and encouraging them to submit job applications to the company.

**Sources for Hiring**

Basically, there are two categories of sources used for recruitment:

1. Internal resources

2. External sources

Employees who are currently employed by the company are considered internal sources. The following may be found in the internal sources:

(a) Promotion and Transfer

(b) Internal notification

**Benefits of using internal sources for hiring:**

**1.** The benefit of hiring from within is that candidates are already familiar with the corporate culture.

**2.** We can rely on our staff since they have been tried and tested.

**3.** It gives workers a helpful signal and reassurance that their services are valued, which keeps them motivated and positive.

4. Because it provides workers with a sense of job security and chance for progress, it lowers labour turnover.
5. Since our staff members are well-versed in the company, less work training is necessary.
6. Compared to other sources, internal sources of hiring are less expensive.

## Benefits of using internal sources for hiring:

Internal sources of hiring have some drawbacks, which include:

1. It restricts the options to a small number of workers.
2. When choosing an employee, the preferences of superiors are a major consideration.
3. The personnel who are not chosen become frustrated as a result.

## Outside Resources for Hiring:

These are not internal sources of the company. They could originate from the following sources:

a) Commercials/ Advertising
b) Workplace Trade-Ins
c) Recruitment on campus
d) Uninvited candidates
e) Contractors for labour
f) Referrals from employees and
g) Field excursions

(a) Advertising: The most widely utilized strategy is placing advertisements in trade journals, magazines, and newspapers. An advertisement needs to be well-written to be successful. If it is not written correctly, it might not attract the suitable kind of applications or it might draw in an excessive number of unqualified candidates. The following four fundamental processes should be included in any well-designed advertising copy:

1. Getting Noticed
2. Growing Interest
3. Creating Want and
4. Creating Movement.

This four-step process is known as the AIDA formula. The pulling effect of advertising material must be maximized by paying special attention to appropriate pulls or appeals. At this point, image building can be made effective because advertisements are how prospective applicants are initially introduced to the organization.

There are three categories or approaches to advertising those businesses use. They're as follows:

1. Utilizing Post Box Numbers: - Some businesses run their own advertising campaigns. The company name and address are absent from this advertisement; all that is shown is a post box number. However, good applicants who believe it is worthwhile to apply for a job without knowing the prospective company should generally avoid using this strategy.

2. Using Specialized Agencies: - Some businesses don't run their own advertising campaigns. They utilize specialized agencies that post job openings without disclosing the identity of their customer.

3. Direct Advertising: - Certain organizations carry out their own advertising, including their names and addresses. This direct approach is recommended since it gives applicants insight into the specific organization they are applying to.

(b) Trades in Employment. Employment exchanges keep track of jobless candidates' names, qualifications, and other details by registering them. Government employment exchanges and commercial employment agencies are the two categories of employment exchanges.

(c) Campus Recruitment: Recruiters are occasionally dispatched to schools, where they meet with the placement officer or faculty members who suggest qualified applicants. Campus recruitment is one of the main sources for this system's prevalence in the United States. Nonetheless, Indian firms are starting to take an interest in the concept of campus recruitment.

(d) Unsolicited applications: These provide an additional source. Some applicants submit their applications even in the absence of an invitation from the company.

(e) Labour Contractors: - To hire employees, many businesses use labour contractors. This approach is typically used when the work is just temporary in nature.

(f) Employee referrals: - Current employees' friends and

family can also be a valuable source for hiring new staff members. Certain companies with a positive personnel relations history encourage their staff members to recommend qualified applicants for different positions within the company.

(g) Field Trips: - A team conducting interviews visits towns and cities that are recognised to have the kind of workers needed. The candidates are informed in advance of their arrival dates, as well as the time and location of the interview.

## Benefits of using outside sources for hiring:

1. The organization gains new skill and talent.
2. New hires might attempt to break traditional routines.
3. Under the organization's terms and conditions, new hires may be chosen.
4. Highly skilled and seasoned workers could contribute to improved performance inside the company.
5. The greatest choice may be made since candidates are chosen from a wide pool of candidates. Put another way, the recruiter has a large pool of potential prospects to pick from.
6. An organization can obtain the necessary staff from external sources, who possess the necessary expertise and standard.
7. Because potential employees don't require additional training to enhance their skills, external sources of recruiting are cost-effective.

**Benefits of using outside sources for hiring:**

1. Employee morale is lowered by external recruitment sources since outsiders are favoured to fill better positions.

2. Employees cannot grow in their careers because of external recruitment sources.

3. Due to the limited amount of time at his disposal, the recruiter might not be able to adequately assess outside applicants. This could lead to poor personnel selection.

4. The organization's policies and practices are not fully understood by outsiders. As a result, they ought to receive costly instruction.

**Employment Guidelines**

A policy is a standing plan; policies are instructions that offer an ongoing framework for executive decisions regarding ongoing management issues. While policies aid in decision-making, there may be times when exceptions and extraordinary situations call for modifications. Such a policy states the goals of the hiring process and offers a framework for carrying out the hiring process through procedures.

**The following is a list of essentials for policy formation:**

1. A policy must be unambiguous, affirmative, and specific. Everyone in the company needs to understand it.
2. A policy ought to be implementable in real life.

3. A policy ought to be both highly permanent and flexible at the same time.

4. It is necessary to create a policy that addresses all plausible predicted circumstances.

5. A policy should be based on reasoned analysis and factual information.

6. Laws, rules, and economic concepts should all be followed by a policy.

## A policy ought to be a broad summary of the accepted rule:

Thus, a thoughtful and well-thought-out hiring policy that is based on business objectives and needs can assist the company choose the correct kind of employees and prevent rash judgements.

Therefore, an organization's dedication to values like these is reflected in its recruitment policy.

(i) To identify and hire the most competent candidates for every position.

(ii) Provide lifetime employment to attract and retain top people; and

(iii) Promote personal development among employees.

## Selection

The purpose of selection, whether internal or external, is for the organization to consciously choose a predetermined number of employees from a vast pool of candidates. Selecting individuals who have the highest likelihood of staying with the organization and performing their duties as effectively as possible is the major goal of employee selection. Consequently, the process of selection aims to identify a qualified applicant for the position. Naturally, this results in many applications being turned down. Selection becomes a negative function as a result. Recruitment is a positive function in a contract since it aims to increase the number of people that submit job applications.

## Procedure Steps for Selection

1. Bank of applications.
2. Initial discussion with the applicant.
3. Job assessments.
4. Conversations.
5. Verifying references.
6. Medical or physical assessment.
7. The last interview and the orientation.

Interview: - The organization will schedule an initial interview with those who are chosen for one based on the information provided in the application bank. This is to assess the candidate's look, build a cordial rapport between the candidate and the organization, and get further information to provide clarification on the data that is already on the application sheet. An interview is a personal, observational, face-to-face assessment technique used to assess an applicant. Its goal is not to thoroughly investigate applicants' qualifications, but rather to reject applications from those who are unable to find work due to age, physical disabilities, or a lack of necessary experience or training. A preliminary interview becomes essential when a high volume of applicants is received for the position.

Employment tests: During the selection process, several tests are utilized to get a deeper understanding of a candidate's character and skills. To estimate a candidate's ability, IQ, etc., psychologists have created a variety of tests. The various test kinds are as follows:

(a) Test of aptitude: Tests of aptitude, also known as potential ability tests, are frequently used to gauge a candidate's aptitude for picking up new skills or jobs. Ability and talents are measured by aptitude exams. They let us to determine whether an applicant is qualified for a position, should they be hired. Particular aptitude tests have been created for vocations requiring physical, mechanical, and administrative skills and abilities. There are aptitude tests available for practicing law, medicine, painting, and other professions. Aptitude tests have the drawback of not measuring motivation.

(b) Interest test: This is a tool used to determine the kind of work that a candidate is interested in. An interest test only reveals a candidate's interest in a specific position. It doesn't demonstrate his aptitude for it.

(c) Intelligence test: This assessment measures the candidate's mental capacity. This test is used to evaluate the candidate's mental alertness, capacity for reasoning, comprehension, etc. Although opinions on this vary, aptitude tests are typically included in intelligence testing. Typically, intelligence test results are presented as

Intelligence Quotient (IQ), which is determined by the following formula:-

Mental Age / Actual Age multiplied by 100 is IQ.

Tests of intelligence can be used to evaluate candidates and predict an employee's future in terms of word fluency, memory, inductive reasoning, and perceptive speed.

(d) Performance or achievement test: In the event that the candidate is ultimately chosen, this test is meant to gauge his degree of expertise in the specific trade or occupation to which he will be assigned. Achievement tests evaluate the information and skills that a candidate has gained from prior instruction or experience.

(e) Personality test: A personality test is used to gauge a candidate's traits that make up their personality. Personality assessments play a crucial role in the hiring process, especially when candidates are appointed to positions as supervisors or higher executives.

Interview: All candidates who pass the examinations after putting them through different kinds of assessments will eventually be invited for an interview. The interview process is arguably the most complex and challenging aspect of the hiring process. The purpose of interviews is to evaluate a candidate's suitability for a certain position. It evaluates his intelligence, general perception, experience, skill, mental and psychological reactions, ability to perceive things rapidly, and capacity to make snap decisions. Probably the most popular method of selection is the interview. This method of selection allows the employer to see the candidate as a whole and evaluate the candidate's actions immediately.

The interview is an exchange between the interviewer and the candidate. When used appropriately, it can be a very effective method for obtaining precise information and access to content that would not otherwise be possible. Inadequate interview management can contribute to bias by limiting or warping the flow of information. Thus, the purpose of an interview is to get as much information as possible from the candidate about his suitability for the position being considered. The following lists the many interview formats used for selection:

a) Initial interview
b) In-depth conversation
c) Interview stress
d) Talk-based interview
e) Formal interview
f) Unstructured conversation
g) Interview in a group
h) Last-minute interview

(a) Initial interview: This type of interview serves as a screening tool for candidates to determine whether a more in-depth discussion is warranted. This method's only justification is that it saves the business money and time. A thorough explanation of the preliminary or initial interview is provided in point (2) above.

(a) Comprehensive interview: - Comprehensive interviews, also known as depth interviews, go into the applicant's entire life experience. It is semi-structured and includes questions in important areas that the interviewer has researched beforehand. The purpose of this type of interview is to gain a true understanding of the interviewee by closely investigating his background and thought process in order to make an informed assessment and decision. It's a great way to choose executive candidates. But, in the end, it takes a lot of time.

(c) Stress interviews are intentional attempts to apply pressure in order to see how an applicant handles pressure. In order to create tension, the interviewer reacts to the applicant's responses with a barrage of sharp follow-up questions or with wrath, silence, and criticism. There are new events including noise, disruptions, and timetable changes.

(d) Discussion Interview: During this kind of interview, candidates engage in group conversations while understanding that the session is a test, but they are unsure of the specific traits being evaluated.

(e) Structured Interview: This type of interview is predicated on the idea that, in order to be as successful as possible, every detail should be found. There must be very minimal variation in the sequence in which the questions are asked.

(f) Unstructured Interview: During the unstructured interview, the candidate will be asked a series of broad questions to which he is free to respond in any manner that suits him. The candidate is urged to express himself freely in this kind of interview. Finding characteristics, strengths, weaknesses, etc. is the goal.

(h) Final Interview: It's best to pitch the position to the chosen candidate after they've been chosen. It is important to give him a sense of his potential moving forward in the company. By giving him an appointment letter or signing a service agreement with him, you can formally appoint him. The terms and conditions of employment, salary scale, and other perks related to the position are included in the appointment letter.

7. Final Interview and Onboarding: - The management will need to persuade the chosen candidate to accept the position after he has been officially chosen. It is important to inform him of his responsibilities, expectations, and future opportunities inside the company.

## Different Induction Programme Types

1. General Induction Programme: - The procurement function reaches its conclusion once an offer of employment is extended and accepted. The person must therefore have an eastern perspective on their work and the company.

2. Particular orientation programme: - The foreman is in charge of induction at this point. The foreman must possess specified skills in order to complete the induction. Operational expertise relevant to the position and area must be given to a new hire. Every new hire ought to be aware of

(i) The individuals you collaborate with.

(ii) The tasks that fall under your purview.

(iii) The outcome that you achieve.

(iv) The work's present state.

(v) The connections you have within the company.

(vi) Records and reports that you need to keep track of and comprehend.

## Training And Development

Training and development is a subsystem amongst the various other functions of HRM being practiced in any organization. It ensures reduction of randomness and learning or behavioral change takes place in structured format. Training generally is a transforming procedure which requires some input and in turn it produce outputs in the form of knowledge, skills and attitudes. It can be defined as any attempt to improve the current or future performance of an employee by increasing his/her ability to high delivery of performance through learning and changing the employee's attitude towards work or increasing his/her skills and job knowledge.

Importance of Training and development for the organization

There are many benefits of Training and Development to any organization as well as employees of that organization which can be categorized under the following heads viz-

1) **Benefits for the organization:**

- Improvement in profitability for the organization.
- Improvement in the job knowledge and skills at all levels.

- Improves the morale of the work force and a better corporate image.
- Better understanding and carrying out of organizational policies.
- Development in the leadership skills, motivation and loyalty while better attitudes keep down costs in many areas e.g. production, personnel and administration.
- Reduction in outside consulting costs by the utilization of competent internal consulting.

## 2) Benefits for the individual:

- Greater self development and self confidence.
- Implementing training program the motivational variables of recognition, achievement, growth, responsibility and advancement are internalized and can also be undertaken.
- Employees are better freed of tension, stress, conflict and frustration.
- Employees can aid a rational avenue for growth.
- Elimination of fear in attending new task can be evident.
- Development in speaking and listening skills along with interpersonal skills.

## The Training Process Model

**Assessment phase:**

- Organizational Objectives and Strategies.
- Identification of Learning and Training Needs/Training Needs Analysis.

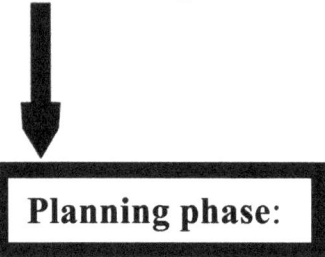

**Planning phase:**

- Creating Training Budget
- Design training program
- Devising methods and modes of training

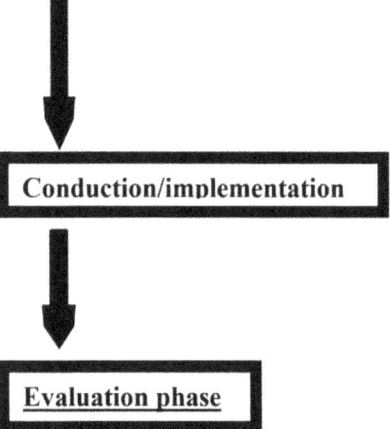

- Evaluation of training program

- Check- objective are achieved

Organizational Objectives and Strategies:

The evaluation of an organization's goals and plans, such as what the business is and what caliber of goods or services should be provided, is the first stage in the training process. What position does this business want to have in the near future? The training programme is developed more quickly and with clear guidelines because the objectives are tailored to the demands of the individual. Training objectives outline the expectations for the learner at the conclusion of the programme.

## HR Accounting And Audit

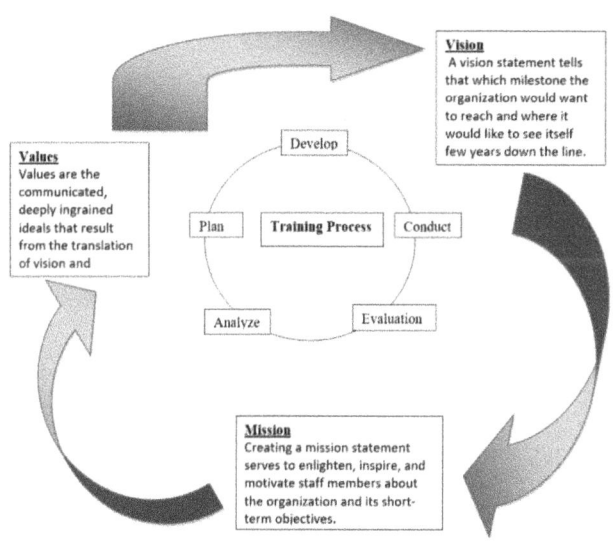

## Conduction/Implementation Phase

A list of all the names of employees should be first collected with their designations and department and then a proper day needs to be scheduled with date and time along with the finalization of the venue. All the employees should be made aware of the same.

The training program needs to be conducted and completed as per the schedule. Certain aspects are very important while conduction of a training program like where is the training going to be conducted and how to which probable answers could be like at the job itself; on site but not the job for example in a training room in the company or off site such as a university, college classroom, hotel, etc. Next comes the question of timing of the training program like what will be the supposed length/duration of the training program and whether the company would be comfortable enough to provide that much of time for the training program to be conducted. Answers to all the queries as above will lead to a proper conduction of the training program as per schedule. Moreover continuous monitoring is required for the training flow in a scheduled way and to ensure that it does not cross the training budget.

Evaluation Phase

After completion of training, feedback needs to be taken from the participant about the trainers and after a gap of considerable period feedback needs to be gathered of the concerned participant about his improvement in his skill or the degree to which his/her knowledge is enhanced. After the individual feedback is received by the trainees, an After Training Result should be generated and forwarded to the immediate superior. It is the duty of the concerned superior to prepare an Improvement chart which would be an indication of how well the training has been achieved by the trainee.

## TYPES OF TRAINING

### A) ON JOB TRAINING:

**1) Job Instruction Training:**

It is the training procedure that involves incremental learning. Typically, an experienced trainer identifies the stages required for the task and exposes an employee to each phase. A significant number of managers place a high emphasis on the benefits of gaining experience through work. They like this approach because, in contrast to other formal training approaches, it provides learners direct accountability. It is important to keep in mind that although doing is the best way for people to learn, workout regimens should be carefully thought out and organized.

**2) Vestibule Training:**

This technique replicates a work environment using technology and equipment that is comparable to those used in real production or operation, but it is done off-site. Separate from the main manufacturing area is a designated room or area for special operations. Under the given circumstances, the student is allowed to learn without interfering with current operations. Vestibule training relieves the employee of the burden of having to produce while learning, which is one of its main benefits.

This kind of training has the drawback that it is hard to replicate the demands and realities of real-world decision-making in the workplace. An additional drawback is having to hire a specialized trainer and duplicate facilities.

### 3) Programmed Instruction:

This approach provides instruction without the help of a trainer. The trainee receives information in blocks, either through a teaching machine or a book. Each block of content is read, and then the student is required to respond to a question regarding it. Programme initiation thus entails... (1) Asking inquiries (ii) giving the individual a chance to reply; (iii) giving feedback on the accuracy of his or her response; and (iv) moving on to the next block if the responses are accurate.

### 4) Induction:

A newly hired employee need to be greeted as a new member of the organization prior to receiving training for the particular position. The majority of people have vivid memories of their first day of work. For this reason, a proper induction is essential to the training procedure. It allows new hires to reap the full benefits of on-the-job training by making them feel comfortable more quickly. Three components make up a quality induction programme. (i) General information provided informally or during a group meeting in the HR division. (ii) Additional details regarding departmental facilities and requirements provided by the department's superior. (iii) A follow-up interview a few weeks after the employee starts work, conducted by the supervisor or a personal/HR department representative, to address any queries the new hire may have and to reiterate some of the previously discussed material for clarity.

## 5) Apprentice:

This is advantageous for businesses that depend on a steady stream of new hires hoping to become all-around artisans, like the building and construction, printing, and metalworking industries. This type of training is costly because it involves a lengthy programme and ongoing supervision. In unionized workplaces, union acceptance is a requirement of the apprentice agreement, which defines strict standards.

## 6) Job Rotation:

In this kind of training, tasks are typically rotated among staff members who work in different departments but are generally employed in the same category or hierarchy. Employees that work in multiple departments are periodically familiar with the specific goals and demands of each department. This training has improved the employee's productivity and understanding of a variety of trades.

## B) OFF JOB TRAINING

1 Simulation: Simulation replicates real-world conditions that arise in the course of work. It's an effort to give a learner a realistic decision-making environment. The trainee is presented with potential problem scenarios and choice options through simulation. Two crucial simulation methods are role-playing and case studies (a, b).

## a) Case Study

This text provides a written account of a real-life business scenario that makes the reader wonder what's really happening, what the situation or problems are, and what action is best. These cases, which are drawn from actual organizational experiences, are an attempt to explain actual issues that managers have encountered. Trainees examine the cases to identify issues, evaluate them, come up with several solutions, pick the best one, and put it into practice.

## b) Role Play:

Instead of real problems, it usually concentrates on emotional or interpersonal ones. The basic idea behind role playing is to set up a case study or other realistic scenario and then assign the trainees to play the roles of various personalities in it. For instance, a male employee might pretend to be a female advisor, and a female supervisor might pretend to be a male employee. After that, a typical work scenario might be shown to them, and they would be asked to react accordingly. Improved comprehension is one of the outcomes, among others. The participants in the role play should gain firsthand knowledge of the scenarios they encounter in their daily lives or at work. It is crucial that it accurately depicts the participants' actual working circumstances. There is room for the participants to grow into their roles, even though they are prescribed by scripts. The role plays, the guidelines for participating in them, and the dos and don'ts for the role players must be explained to the entire group. Three categories of role plays exist: One can engage in simple role play, multiple role play, reverse role play, or both.

**Steps for Arranging a Role Play**

(i) Determine the issue.

(ii) Create the role play's framework.

(iii) Giving each person a role.

(iv) Creating the exercise's supplies.

(v) Laying down the stage.

(vi) Outlining standard operating procedures.

(vii) Briefing on roles.

2) Sensitivity training: The organization makes an effort to include individuals from many divisions. There are about fifteen spots available. They are removed from their place of residence. There is lodging available in a different training facility. The training programme lasts for around two weeks. In the training hall, every participant gathers. This place does not have a trainer on hand. Participants begin interacting with one another after being grouped. They gradually engage in more conversation regarding the business. The facilitator is in attendance. He or she encourages them to participate in the exchange. It is a process of personal development through perception. When they return to the initial organisational setting, their attitude changes. Improving interpersonal relationships is one of the training's main goals. This results in the organization's internal growth and an enhancement of the workplace culture. The

facilitator, who enjoys coordinating the training process by engaging as a participant, is ultimately responsible for this situation's success.

3) MBO, or management by goals The key training technique known as "management by objective" or "management by result" was developed by Peter Drucker. It is a crucial OD intervention strategy. This procedure aims to increase the organization's efficacy and assemble a team from several areas. Superiors sit with subordinates during this process and make decisions together. During a collaborative decision-making process, the team attempts to determine key result areas (KRA). These are the areas in which each specific department can increase or improve upon its effectiveness. There is a time limit on this programme. It is therefore time-bound. In other words, MBO is the process by which superiors and subordinates collaborate to determine a quantifiable, measurable, time-bound programme to be implemented in each of their main outcome areas. MBO has five goals, which are S M A R T. These are time-bound, goal-oriented, quantifiable, attainable, and specified.

4) Audio Visuals: These consist of films, video tapes, overheads, and television slides. These can be utilized to give a variety of time-condensed, realistic examples of work environments and scenarios. However, the communication is one-way.

5) Group Discussion: This might happen when everyone in the group sits down to talk about a certain subject. The goal of a group discussion is for participants to share knowledge, ideas, and perspectives in an organized yet

casual setting about any subject or issue. All of the contributions are combined and evaluated for their applicability and relevance to the discussion's goals.

6) Management: Game a management game is a kind of instruction that focuses on particular facets of administration or business. It's a simulated exercise meant to mimic the limitations and demands of the participants' regular workplace. The participants receive knowledge about the marketing, finance, human resources, and other aspects of an organization's operations. They are organized into functional teams to oversee operations and take into account the flow of events and issues. Dealing with people, making decisions, and solving problems are all part of the role. Each team makes a choice based on the data and information at its disposal, keeping in mind the general guidelines and game objectives. The group evaluates the decision's results in view of how they will impact the current circumstances and ongoing events. The trainer feeds back the decisions' consequences back to the squad. The group then moves on to make more decisions in response to the evolving events, circumstances, and scenario. Thus, a business game makes an effort to combine several aspects of real-world decision-making.

7) Brainstorming During the brainstorming phase, the management poses a real challenge. Subordinates are then presented with the problem and asked to come up with solutions and suggestions for making decisions. No matter how broad the ideas are, the management accepts them all in the first instance. The next step is for management to prioritize the three or four good ideas. Finally, management decides which ideas are most

appropriate after considering how they will affect the culture of the company.

The first step in brainstorming is idea generation.

(i) Modifying concepts.

(ii) Putting every concept up on the Flipchart.

(iii) Examining concepts and their implications.

(iv) Selecting the ideal concept and making an action plan.

8) Lecture By definition, the lecture consists of the trainer's words. Thus, it is a medium of spoken symbols. This is the most traditional form of instruction, when the instructor directly and unilaterally provides the material verbally to the class based on her knowledge and experience in that sector. It suggests one-way communication quite obviously. The lecture's goal as a training tool is, in fact, narrowly focused. The lecture method works best in situations when it facilitates the transmission of intellectual understanding as a necessary component of the learning process, within the continuum of information, understanding, knowledge, skills, behaviour, and attitudes. A lecture is not helpful for changing behaviour or improving abilities, although it might be beneficial for imparting knowledge. The instructor shouldn't be afraid to use visual aids to highlight and emphasize a subject. It is also possible to give out handouts to enhance learning.

# Sustainable Development

**Sustainable Development**: Development that meets the needs of the present without compromising the ability of future generations to meet their own needs.

**Key Concept**: Balance among economic growth, environmental health, and social equity.

**Origins**: Popularized by the 1987 Brundtland Report, also known as "Our Common Future."

## Three Pillars of Sustainable Development

### 1  Economic Sustainability

Efficient and responsible use of resources.

Long-term economic growth without negatively impacting social, environmental, and cultural aspects.

Innovation and investments in sustainable industries.

### 2  Environmental Sustainability

Protection and conservation of natural resources.

Reduction of pollution and waste.

Use of renewable resources and energy.

Conservation of biodiversity and ecosystems.

### 3  Social Sustainability

Ensuring equitable access to resources and opportunities.

Promoting social inclusion and cohesion.

Respect for human rights and cultural diversity.

Enhancing quality of life and well-being.

**Key Principles**

**Intergenerational Equity**: Fairness to future generations.

**Precautionary Principle**: Preventive measures when there is risk of serious harm.

**Integration**: Interconnection of economic, social, and environmental goals.

**Participation**: Involvement of all stakeholders, including marginalized groups.

- Sustainable Development Goals (SDGs) are adopted by the United Nations in 2015.

**17 Goals** address global challenges including poverty, inequality, climate change, environmental degradation, peace, and justice.

- Challenges to Sustainable Development

**Resource Depletion**: Overuse of natural resources.

**Climate Change**: Impact of global warming on ecosystems and human societies.

**Economic Inequality**: Disparities in wealth and access to resources.

**Political Instability**: Governance issues that hinder sustainable policies.

**Technological Gaps**: Unequal access to sustainable technologies.

- Strategies for Sustainable Development

**Green Technologies**: Adoption of renewable energy sources, waste recycling, and energy-efficient systems.

**Policy and Legislation**: Government policies promoting sustainability (e.g., carbon pricing, environmental regulations).

**Education and Awareness**: Increasing public understanding of sustainability issues.

**Corporate Responsibility**: Encouraging businesses to adopt sustainable practices.

**International Cooperation**: Collaborative efforts between countries and international organizations.

The concept of a post-2015 development agenda was introduced in the documentary "Future We Want," which was broadcast at the Rio G 20 meeting. The Millennium Development Goals were replaced with the Sustainable Development Goals (SDGs), an intergovernmental agreement designed to serve as the post-2015 development agenda.

The Open Working Group on Sustainable Development objectives of the United Nations General Assembly suggested a set of 17 objectives, 169 targets, and 304 indicators, to be accomplished by 2030. Following deliberations, the United Nations Sustainable Development Summit accepted the "Transforming Our World: the 2030 Agenda for Sustainable Development" agenda. The Rio+20 summit, which took place in Rio de Janeiro in 2012, produced the non-binding Sustainable Development Goals (SDGs).

## The following is a list of the 17 Sustainable Development Goals:

Eliminate poverty worldwide in all of its manifestations.

Put an end to poverty, provide food security, boost nutrition, and advance sustainable agriculture

Make sure everyone has a healthy life and is encouraged to be well at all times.

Make sure that everyone has access to high-quality, inclusive education, and encourage lifelong learning opportunities.

Realize gender parity and give all women and girls more power.

Provide everyone with access to affordable, dependable, sustainable, and modern energy; ensure that water and sanitation are available and managed sustainably; and encourage long-term, inclusive, and sustainable economic growth, full-time employment, productive employment, and decent work for everyone.

Developed robust infrastructure, encouraged equitable and sustainable industrialization, and stimulated innovation

Lessen disparities both within and across nations

Make human settlements and cities robust, safe, inclusive, and sustainable.

Assure a sustainable structure of production and consumption.

Act quickly to mitigate the effects of climate change.

Seas, oceans, and marine resources should be preserved and used responsibly.

Combat desertification, preserve, restore, and encourage the sustainable use of terrestrial ecosystems, sustainably managed forests, stop and reverse land degradation, and stop the loss of biodiversity.

Encourage open and peaceful societies for long-term growth, ensure that everyone has access to justice, and create inclusive, accountable, and successful institutions at all levels.

bolster implementation strategies and revitalise the international alliance for sustainable development

## The status of India's implementation of the Sustainable Development Goals

The Mahatma Gandhi National Rural Employment Guarantee Act (MNREGA) is being put into effect to raise the standard of living and give unskilled labourers' jobs.

The National Food Security Act is being implemented to offer food grains at a reduced cost.

The primary initiative of the Indian government, Swachh Bharat Abhiyan, is to eradicate open defecation in India.

In order to lessen reliance on fossil fuels and take use of renewable energy sources like wind and solar power, 175 GW of renewable energy must be generated by 2022.

The Heritage City Development and Augmentation Yojana (HRIDAY) and Atal Mission for Rejuvenation and Urban Transformation (AMRUT) programmes have been introduced to enhance the infrastructure components.

India has indicated that it intends to ratify the Paris Agreement in order to fight climate change.

Candidates who are getting ready for the upcoming IAS exam should go to the article that is linked for additional information on the test.

**The Millennium Development Goals**

In September 2000, the United Nations mandated that all of its members adhere to a set of eight time-bound benchmarks, known as the Millennium Development Goals, which were expected to be completed within fifteen years. The following list includes the eight goals that make up the Millennium Development Goal:

To achieve universal primary education, reduce severe poverty and hunger, advance gender equality, and empower women

In order to lower the death rate of children

To enhance the health of mothers

To fight against malaria, HIV/AIDS, and other illnesses

To guarantee the sustainability of the environment

to create an international development partnership

The UN received a final report in 2015 that detailed the benefits of the Millennium Development Goal based on the eight criteria and the rate of maternal death. After the MDG's 15-year target was reached, the Sustainable

Development Goal's 17 targets became the basis for development responsibilities.

## 2020 Report on Sustainable Development Goals

The Sustainable Development Goals Report 2020 was made public on July 7, 2020. The research claims that the COVID-19 epidemic caused an unprecedented crisis, which further hampered the advancement of the SDGs. The main ideas from the SDG report are listed below:

There have been improvements in a number of areas, including enhancing the health of mothers and children, boosting access to electricity, and raising the representation of women in government.

The first increase in global poverty since 1998 is predicted to occur in 2020, when an estimated 71 million people are predicted to fall back into extreme poverty. Loss of work is thought to be the primary cause of this, and even those who were previously secure may now be at risk of becoming impoverished.

During the crisis, an estimated 1.6 million workers who were considered vulnerable were either unemployed or underemployed globally, and their earnings were predicted to have decreased by 60%.

During the epidemic, the populations most impacted were women, children, and those living in slums.

Over 370 million children have missed out on the school meals they depend on because of school closures, which have kept 90% of kids globally (1.57 billion) out of the classroom.

The likelihood of child labour and human trafficking has increased due to incidences of poverty, unemployment, and risk to lives.

In addition to the previously mentioned problems, the report indicates that the rate of climate change is still far faster than predicted. The warmest decade, from 2010 to 2019, came to an end in 2019, which was the second-warmest year on record.

**Effects of the MDG and SDG**

The United Nations members used the Millennium Development Goals as a springboard to search for a more developed and promising future for their nations and their citizens. The Millennium Development Goals (MDGs) were approved in 2000, and the 2015 final report included explicit reference to lowering the infant mortality rate, reducing poverty, providing safe drinking water, increasing sanitation, and significantly enhancing people's mental health.

The Sustainable Development Goals aim to improve living conditions worldwide by 2030, following in its footsteps. The plan was approved in 2015, and reports from the UNDP up until 2020 demonstrate the numerous steps that have been done to enhance the nation and the standard of living for people everywhere.

The Sustainable Development Goals have improved people's health, decreased poverty, decreased the rate of maternal death, raised public knowledge of both communicable and non-communicable diseases, and highlighted the importance of childhood vaccinations. In addition to efforts to improve global access to medication, mental illness is becoming recognized as a serious concern.

All things considered, the Sustainable Development Goals aim to improve the world by eliminating poverty, enhancing health, creating jobs, empowering women, lowering inequality, and achieving all seventeen of the UN's set targets within the allotted 15 years.

## Questions

| Select the option that the process by which the aptitudes, skills and abilities of employees to perform specific jobs are increased | Training | Induction | Orientation | Performance appraisal | 1 |
|---|---|---|---|---|---|
| Select the option that the group which participates in sensitivity training | Training group | Conflicting group | Transactional group | None of these | 3 |
| Select the option that shows | Individual | Team intervention | Organisational | None of these | 3 |

| | | | | | |
|---|---|---|---|---|---|
| example of Management Development Programme (MDP) | intervention | | intervention | | |
| Select the option that express other two stages next to unfreezing stage in Kurt Lewin's change model | Moving | Refreezing | Neither (Moving) nor (Refreezing) | Both (Moving) and (Refreezing) | 4 |
| Select the option that shows the key component in Training games & Simulations | Challenges | Rules | Interactivity | All | 4 |
| Select the option that where from communication begins with- | encoding | idea origination | decoding | channel selection | 2 |
| Select the option that is expected to last in the long run | Low productivity | High morale | Both 'A' and 'B' | None of these | 2 |

| Select the option where problem solving skills are more related to | Training | Networking | Decision making | Appraisal | 3 |
|---|---|---|---|---|---|
| Select the option that where separate room is created to cope up with organizational situation. | Vestibule school | Case study | Experiential learning | Lecture Method | 1 |
| Choose name for vertical job loading | Job analysis | Job enrichment | Job evaluation | Job enlargement | 2 |
| Choose the activity of efficient manager | Understand human behaviour | Predict human behaviour | Control human behaviour | All of these | 4 |
| Choose the acronym KRA | Key recruitment areas | Key result areas | Key remuneration areas | None of these | 2 |
| Choose from following terms that refers to the process of | Recruitment | Employee selection | Performance appraisal | Employee orientation | 3 |

| | | | | | |
|---|---|---|---|---|---|
| evaluating an employee's current and/or past performance relative to his or her performance standards | | | | | |
| Select from the option the primary purpose of providing employees with feedback during a performance appraisal | Apply for managerial positions | Remove any performance deficiencies | Revise their performance standards | Enroll in work-related training programs | 2 |
| In most organizations, choose the person who is primarily responsible for appraising an employee's performance | Employee's direct supervisor | Company appraiser | Human resources manager | EEO representative | 1 |
| Select from the following that is NOT one of the | Assigning specific goals | Assigning measura | Assigning challenging but | Administering consequences for | 4 |

| recommended guidelines for setting Effective employee goals | | ble goals | doable goals | failure to meet goals | |
|---|---|---|---|---|---|
| Choose the acronym SMART goals | Specifi, measurable, attainle, relevan, and timely | Straight forward, meaningful, accessible, real, and tested | Strategic, moderate, achievable, relevant, and timely | Specific, measurable, achievable, relevant, and tested | 1 |

| |
|---|
| Interpret sustainable development. |
| Interpret HRD. |
| Explain vestibule method as one on job training method. |
| Explain MBO. |
| Explain sensitivity training. |
| Explain the term 'job rotation'. |
| Explain advantages of training. |

## References:

1 Essential Economics for Business (formerly Economics and the Business Environment), Jones, Elizabeth; Sloman, John, Pearson Education Limited Pearson, Year: 2017.

2. Economic Environment of Business: Theory & The Indian Case, Adhikary, M, Sultan Chand & Sons, Year: 2012.

3. Business Environment, Shaikh, Saleem, Pearson Education, Year: 2010.

4. Essentials of Business Environment, Aswathappa, K, Himalaya Publishing House, Year: 2017.

5. Indian Economy: Performance and Policies, Kapila, Uma, Academic Foundation, Year: 2021.

6. The International Business Environment, Morrison, J, Macmillan Education, Year: 2020.

7. Economic Reforms and the Indian Economy, Balakrishnan, Pulapre, Oxford University Press, Year: 2010.

8. Business Environment in a Global Context, Ho, R, Oxford University Press, Year: 2014.

www.ingramcontent.com/pod-product-compliance
Lightning Source LLC
LaVergne TN
LVHW061542070526
838199LV00077B/6875